AHEAD

OF THE

CHAINS

BUSINESS LEADERSHIP INSIGHTS
FROM THE GAME OF FOOTBALL

INSTALLING YOUR SYSTEM

ooooooooooooooooooooooooooooooooooooooooooooooooooooooooooooooooo

BY MATT PROSTKO

Printed in the United States of America

First Printing, 2017

ISBN 978-0-9996441-2-6

Written by Matt Prostko
www.AheadoftheChains.com

TABLE
OF
CONTENTS

INTRODUCTION

I love the game of football. While I have loved it since I was a kid, I have grown to appreciate it even more as an adult. In my career as a strategy execution consultant, I work with large enterprises, helping them to accelerate the execution of their strategy. I consult with leadership teams on defining and deploying organizational vision, strategy and culture, creating execution discipline, and developing the leadership talent, environment and skills necessary to drive business results. And all of these elements are also central to American football; no other sport is as focused on strategy, execution and leadership. As such, I began to see football as an interesting metaphor for business leadership, and found valuable insights that informed my work as a consultant.

Reflecting on the game of football, it was obvious to me that certain organizations and coaches consistently outperformed their peers. Regardless of what level – professional, college, or even high school – there were teams that were able to maintain that high level of performance over time. Whether you were looking at one game, one season, or even a decade, certain teams seemed to always be one step ahead of the rest – and I wanted to understand why.

So, I began reading everything I could find about the most successful football coaches and organizations. My experience as a management consultant allowed me to examine their approach to the game, and to leadership in general, from a business perspective. From that angle, I found that the source of their success was not derived from a single stroke of genius, or some secret insight that only they possessed. What consistently separated the best from the rest, was their development of, and a commitment to, an integrated foundational system that they used to guide the team or the organization as a whole. That "system", as football coaches and executives often call it, provides the blueprint for how the organization operates – the goals it sets, the strategies it implements, and the culture that defines its behavior.

Organizations that had an integrated system; one that it defined clearly , that it communicated openly, that led the implementation of it effectively, and that consistently made decisions in accordance with it, significantly outperformed the competition. But again, it wasn't because of some noticeable, outlying performance. They just seemed to be one step ahead of everyone else. They made fewer mistakes. They didn't take backward steps. They didn't waste resources. They didn't make bad personnel decisions. They just demonstrated sound fundamentals, and they were consistently effective. In football parlance, they always seemed to be "ahead of the chains".

For those unfamiliar with the phrase, being "ahead of the chains" in a football game, means that you are executing effectively. It means that you are gaining more yards on every play than the minimum that would is required to keep advancing. For example, you tend to be running plays from 2nd down and 4 yards to go, or 3rd and 1, instead of 2nd and 8, or 3rd and 6. And as such, you give yourself more options, and make it more difficult for the competition to defend you. When teams are playing ahead of the chains, their time on offense increases, and their scoring percentage improves dramatically. The phrase "ahead of the chains" has become synonymous with organizational effectiveness, and in operating your enterprise from an advantaged position.

I get a chance to work with large enterprise clients every day, and essentially, and they hire us to get their organization "ahead of the chains". I work for a somewhat "boutique" consulting organization, BTS USA Inc., that focuses on the execution of strategy through people. After a Fortune 500 company has decided on a new direction, or launched a major initiative, we come in and help them execute it. Not by installing new information systems, or reengineering tools or processes, but by getting their people aligned, prepared and motivated to drive that strategy or initiative forward, and to help their people do the best work of their lives.

More specifically, I consult with organizations to define, refine and align to a clear vision (think "winning aspiration"), build and support a healthy organizational culture (think "team chemistry"), refine, communicate, and teach their unique business models (think offensive or defensive football systems/philosophies), drive strategies to win in the marketplace (think football "game plans"), and help them coach their talent to execute those game plans (just as important in the corporate setting). So, my business is a unique combination of traditional consulting - helping to identify the issues that need to be addressed - and talent development – helping to create the environment and capabilities required to be successful. My teams stay engaged through to the resolution of the issue, not just on submitting a deck describing what is wrong. So we get the rare opportunity to see what actually works, not just what sounds good in a strategy presentation.

Since 2007, I have led engagements with over 20 Fortune 500 companies in industries such as software, oil & gas, information technology, consumer goods, professional services, retail, logistics, semiconductor, and insurance. And while each one of those engagements is unique, ultimately, the rationale for each is the same. My teams and I were there to help them get the results they were looking for – to get "ahead of the chains" - by improving the effectiveness of their human capital.

But, my point of view in this book does not come solely from my consulting experience. Prior to my time at BTS, I spent about 8 years in management roles in the software and semiconductor industry at Motorola and its subsidiaries. Before that, I built, ran, and sold a company that distributed healthcare equipment. I also had brief stints at IBM and PepsiCo. So, my business experience - in these various industries and companies, in both high growth and in imploding markets, in periods of wild success and dismal failure – have all informed my perspectives in this book.

So, what do organizations that play "ahead of the chains" tend to do differently than ones that are less effective? Well if you were hoping that I could distill this down into one sentence, or a quick fix, I am sorry to disappoint you. But, essentially, I can cluster the elements into two primary groupings; Installing Your System, and Executing Your System. I will focus on executing and leading your system in a subsequent book, but here, I will focus on how to design and install your "system" – an integrated set of elements that will form the foundation of your organization. That foundation will allow you to play ahead of the chains and sustainably deliver above average results with an efficient use of resources.

Successful football teams take a careful and thoughtful approach to building that strong foundation. They tend to have a clear vision that engages a broad set of stakeholders in the pursuit of organizational goals. Winning teams have simple strategies that clearly explain how everyone contributes. And, they have an organizational culture that provides an environment that supports the vision and the effective execution of the strategy. These organizations sustain their success, because they have installed an integrated system, wherein the core elements of the system mutually reinforce each other, creating a flywheel effect. That integrated system is the engine that ensures that your organization can operate "ahead of the chains".

So why the football metaphor? Well, I have been around football all my life. I was born in western Pennsylvania, and grew up in Texas, arguably the two biggest bastions of American football. I was born in the late 60s, and was a kid living in Pittsburgh during the Steelers dynasty run of the 1970s. So, I got a chance to see what greatness looked like at an early age. Whether you are a Steeler fan or not, knowledgeable football fans recognize that the Steelers are one of the most consistent and successful franchises in professional football. Since the 1970 merger that defined the modern-day National Football League, they have significantly more wins than any other franchise in a league that is designed to deliver parity.

Over the years, many teams have been able to rise to success, but ultimately fall again, mirroring the cyclical nature of the sport. So, as a fan, I have always been proud of the consistency demonstrated by the Steelers organization. But as a strategy execution consultant, I was intrigued by, and driven to learn how they were able to win consistently, when the league structure is designed to make that very difficult. What does this organization do differently, that allows them to outperform the pull to parity, consistently, over time?

As I mentioned, I did not stay in Pittsburgh. I moved to Texas as a young man and spent my high school years there. I attended a high school that had a rich football tradition. And like most other able-bodied males at that school that did not possess the requisite musical talent to be in the band, I played football. Most everyone has read the books, or watched the television shows or movies, about the passion of Texans for their high school football. While I did not attend Permian High School of "Friday Night Lights" fame, football was woven through the fabric of my school too, and it was the foundation of the social life there. But like the movies, it did not stop with the students. The entire neighborhood was involved, with over 10,000 people showing up on Friday nights for games. That level of support translated to an environment of enthusiasm and success, and a clear winning aspiration that the entire community bought into. As I look back on that, what could be learned about gaining stakeholder support to an organizational vision? Are there lessons that could be applied in engaging customers, suppliers, partners in your vision and goals that could create a competitive advantage for large enterprises?

Unsurprisingly, I passed along my passion for football to my children, especially my eldest son, who also played. He started out playing youth football and enjoyed it, but I looked forward to him playing for the middle school where I felt that he would get a higher level of coaching and development. I was surprised when they were not successful during his years there. The coaches had installed a complex offense that the very young, and inexperienced kids were having significant difficulties with. That translated to a total of one win during his two years of middle school. I did not realize that this was part of a very intentional, and well-thought-out strategy. The middle school was running the full offense that the high school team ran; a pass-oriented spread offense. So, naturally, 12 and 13 year-olds are going to struggle with it. But, during his freshman season at Lake Travis High School, I was able to see the method behind the apparent madness. Those same kids from his middle school went undefeated and won their district. Meanwhile, the varsity team was in the middle of a run of five state championships; the longest stretch in Texas high school football history. Moreover, those five titles were won by three different coaches! The school had created a strategy, and was executing it flawlessly, highlighted by a talent development program that continuously refreshed the organization with prepared players. In global business, if you were experiencing a 25% attrition rate of your best talent every year, and had three different CEO's in five years, you would most likely be hemorrhaging money, and would be on the verge of going under. This was just one example of organizational strategy that successful football teams used to play 'ahead of the chains'. I began to wonder - what lessons could large enterprises learn about strategy from the game of football?

After I graduated high school, I attended the University of Texas, another institution with a rich football tradition. While I had primarily been a fan of professional football up to this point, my time in Austin, Texas introduced me to the passion and pageantry of college sports. Texas had narrowly missed a national championship the year before I arrived, so in my freshman year, they began the year as the #1 ranked team in the country. But midway through the season, the team fell apart. That derailing led to a decay that lasted nearly a decade. The Longhorns were wildly inconsistent, up one year, and down the next; certainly not the elite of college football as their heritage had been.

After three coaches failed to restore The University of Texas to its rightful place in the football landscape, the administration hired Mack Brown. Coach Brown had delivered outstanding success at North Carolina, a storied "basketball school", and had built a top ten football program there, from nothing. After a quick assessment of the program at The University of Texas, Brown realized it was rudderless, and the fan base had grown indifferent. Acting deliberately, he knew he had to create a culture of success for both the organization and the fans, clearly describing what "great" looked like at the University of Texas football program. And through his consistency of communication and action, that culture became reality, and more quickly than anyone could believe. As someone who works with corporate leaders every day, helping them to craft, and carefully curate a corporate culture for their companies, I recognized the significance of that achievement. Upon closer examination, I realized that there were specific lessons that business leaders could extract from Mack Brown's example.

As I said, I love football. And as you may have already surmised, I am passionate about the world of business as well. I read the Business section of the newspaper – yes I am old enough to still read newspapers – with as much fanaticism as I read the Sports section. I have to understand how things work. If my team lost this week, I need to understand if their strategy was flawed, or if it was a failure of execution. Similarly, if one of my clients outperforms their earnings targets, I have dig through it, and understand why.

So, I was compelled to write this book – the intersection between my work life as a business consultant, and my fascination and commitment to be a "student of the game" of football, were so clear to me, that I had to write it down. The metaphors between football and business are powerful, and in this book, I use examples from successful football programs and coaches to impart lessons on executing business strategy. You do not need to be a football fan to understand and enjoy this book. But if you are passionate about being a successful business leader, and are not yet a football fan, I bet you will be after reading it.

I am also an avid reader of other business-focused non-fiction. You will see references to many popular business books that have been published in the last 40 years. Like in the game of football, in business there are very few truly new ideas. The best coaches learn from their peers, and adapt it for their organizations. Most of them end up adding nuances to an already solid platform, innovating off of a core idea, and making it uniquely their own. I consider this book in that light. Quite honestly, there are very few, if any, "ground-breaking" ideas in this book. I am pulling ideas from many sources - at all times crediting the source, of course. Picasso once said, "Good artists copy. Great artists steal." The very best NFL coaches and business leaders have stolen from the people they have learned from. See what you can steal from this book.

I hope to make your larceny simple. As my passion is around business execution, my focus for this book is to help you get results from these insights. Most business books build their narrative based on exhaustive quantitative research that results in some insight that is claimed to be totally unique. Therefore the value in the book is in the secret formula unveiled, that if employed, will help you change your business or your life. I have read a lot of those books, value their contribution, and even refer to several of them and the insights that they offer. However, insights in my opinion are of little value if they are not put to practical use. At all times, this book is focused on communicating and delivering practical tools that you can use in your role as a leader and contributor in your organization. I will close each chapter of the book by distilling the core concepts in the chapter, and to provide simple tools that you can use to put these insights into action for your team or organization.

Using football as a metaphor for business leadership has importance over and above its entertainment value. Football, and sports in general, is a common experience for us all. It is why people bond together around their favorite teams. That experience allows for all parties to share a common feeling or idea together, creating a communication platform that builds a bridge between strangers, and a vocabulary that a group can understand and easily relate to. Football, and its unique vocabulary, have crossed over into popular business culture and lexicon. When things are moving too fast, we often ask for a "time out". When someone makes a mistake, we might yell "Fumble!" in jest. When a situation looks hopeless, we might decide that it is time to "Punt". For that reason, the metaphors, or parables that I use in this book, are there to make the concept I am sharing more approachable. And perhaps, they will be simpler to import into your own business leadership approach, and easier to communicate within your organization.

This book represents a meaningful compilation of research on the leadership topics I have covered, through the lens of some of the great coaches of the modern era of football. Football is unique in that the head coach has more influence over the game than any other sport that I can think of. As such, I read as much as I could find about the coaches that redefined the landscape of the game of football – some with whom you may be familiar with, and some not.

While there have been many great football coaches, who were also great leaders, I was looking for specific attributes. I sought out the principle-based coaches that built lasting organizations based on culture, the "mad scientists" that defined new offensive and defensive strategies, and the detail freaks that held their players to a new standard of execution performance. Each of these archetypes have lessons we can all learn from.

But ultimately, this book isn't really about football. Each sports anecdote or example is simply a metaphor to introduce a new approach to business leadership. I have included both well-known and obscure business case examples that provide direction to the insights and conclusions I share here. Despite my passions that spawned this project, I was continuously surprised at how these two subjects continuously support and provide insights to each other.

The parallels in football and business are significant, not only in content, but in the order in which they are commonly addressed. I have organized the topics in the book, in a business relevant order. I will begin with concepts around Vision, Strategy and Culture, as these elements are foundational for any organization or team. In "coach-speak", this would be referred to as "installing your system", which I think is an appropriate description for businesses as well. In the upcoming second volume, I will turn my attention to Execution and Talent– how to maximize business performance through your system and talent, and to Leadership - how to integrate these ideas into your own personal leadership style and brand.

I will lean on some other football metaphors to help you utilize the insights you gain from the book. Within each chapter, I will call out key learning points as "Coaching Points", helping you refer to these elements easily. I will summarize each chapter in a section called "Chalk Talk", that will include a summary of the fundamental concepts that I discussed, some of the "do's and don'ts", and the key questions for you to consider as you are applying these ideas to your own team or organization. At the end of each section, I will include a "Game Plan" that you can use in your leadership role, to help you execute in the moment.

I hope you enjoy reading the book as much as I did writing it. But as an execution consultant, more than anything, I hope you translate insights from this book into new leadership approaches that drive results for your team or organization.

SECTION I
VISION
SETTING GOALS FOR YOUR SYSTEM

AN INTEGRATED VISION FOR THE ORGANIZATION

On December 5, 2015, Syracuse University hired Dino Babers as their new head football coach. While not necessarily a household name, in general, the Syracuse fan base responded very favorably[1]. After all, he had two consecutive, successful head coaching stops before Syracuse; winning conference championships, playoff games and bowl games in his short stints at Eastern Illinois and Bowling Green. Two days later after his hiring, Babers addressed the media. In less than one minute, he shared his vision for the organization[2]. He began the discussion by asking everyone in the audience to close their eyes. He wanted them all to visualize what he was saying – so they could "see " what he could see so clearly. Here is a partial transcript of that press conference:

> *"You are in the Carrier Dome. The house is filled. The feeling is electric. The noise is deafening. You have a defense that is relentless. You have a special teams which has been well-coached. You have an offense that will not huddle. And you have a game that is faster than you have ever seen on turf. Open your eyes. That is going to be a reality. That is going to be Syracuse football. Thank you"*

[1](Bailey, 2015)
[2](Babers, 2015)

In one simple statement, he created a vision of the future that everyone can understand and rally around. If he is successful in delivering on that vision for the Syracuse program, he will significantly impact the lives of his players and coaches, the financial fortunes of the university and businesses in upstate New York, and the overall happiness of thousands of students, fans and alumni.

Establishing and realizing a compelling vision for a workplace, team or organization can be equally impactful; transforming careers, lives, and fortunes for a wide array of stakeholders. But this is a difficult task for a lot of reasons. Firstly, we can't always have a press conference to tell our story. In large enterprises, we are challenged to create persistent messaging that will be examined and interpreted by many different sets of stakeholders, from many different perspectives.

"You better have a vision, you better have a plan, and you better have the passion for getting things done[3]"

—Lou Holtz, Head Coach,
The University of Notre Dame

Is it a Vision, a Mission, or a Purpose Statement?

Further complicating the matter is the challenge of some basic nomenclature. As someone who helps large enterprise formulate and/or gain alignment around organizational direction, I can confidently say that there is a tremendous amount of confusion around the difference between a Vision statement, a Mission statement, and an organizational Purpose. Definitions vary widely, and consultants and gurus seem vested in, and committed to, making it appear to be as complex as possible.

From my perspective, there is not a lot of value in debating the various definitions, or the way you would use one over another. Each of them

[3](Holtz & McCormick, 2007)

contain important context, and looking at one without the others, can be ineffective. But instead of wasting time creating three unique statements, I prefer to simply condense elements of all of these into one integrated and comprehensive organizational Vision.

■ THE WHAT, WHY & HOW

I mentioned above that Babers had taken an important first step in creating a compelling vision for his organization. I said "first step" because while painting a clear picture of future is critical, it is incomplete. A robust organizational Vision must answer three specific questions; What, Why & How. Or more specifically:

- *What is our destination and what does it look like?*
- *Why should we bother taking the journey, and why would anyone care?*
- *How are we going to get from here to there, and how will we know if we have arrived?*

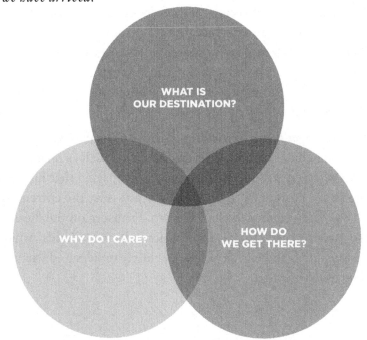

FIGURE 1. ORGANIZATIONAL VISION FRAMEWORK

Each one of these elements is a critical part of the recipe for a fundamentally sound organizational vision, and each has its own unique contribution to creating meaningful engagement to that vision. You could look at these 3 elements through the familiar lens of "Head" (getting intellectual buy-in), "Heart" (getting emotional buy-in), and "Hands" (recruiting incremental behavioral effort). In other words, to be successful, you must engage people through all three of these channels to ensure true adoption of your vision. Consider each element:

- *"What is our destination?"* Executing this element rests primarily on choosing the right destination, and making that destination come to life for your stakeholders by communicating it effectively. Answering this question provides clarity to the "Head", and basic logical understanding of the vision, and makes engagement with the Vision possible.

- *"Why do I care?"* Delivering on this aspect focuses on your purpose for being in existence, over and above winning football games or making money for shareholders. Addressing this concern targets the "Heart", reaching them on an emotional level, and allowing them to power forward when external circumstances challenge the logic of doing so.

- *"How do we get there?"* Providing clarity on the path to the destination includes clarifying several elements such as quantifying the destination with objective metrics, comparing that future state to the current state, and honestly assessing the current gap, and creating urgency to close the gap. Focusing on the measurable goals required to reach the Vision tells the "Hands" what must be done, and allows people to clearly understand what is being asked of them.

Coaching Point: Your Vision should include elements that appeal to the "Head, Heart and Hands" – appealing to logic, creating emotion, and directing the target to action.

These three questions are like the legs on a 3-legged stool. If we are missing any of them, the other two are not of much value. Imagine the scenarios where one of the aspects is absent:

- *Lack of a clear picture of the destination.* Without this, any meaningful engagement is impossible, because no one knows what they are signing up for, and you will be unable to get anyone to commit their "hands" to the work in front of them.

- *Lack of a higher purpose to the Vision.* Without a more meaningful purpose, the attachment to the Vision goes up and down with the won-loss record, or with stock price or bonuses. As soon as there is a better alternative, the "head" will steer people towards that alternative, and away from the Vision.

- *Lack of clear path.* Without clarity around the path to the future state, people are likely to lose "heart" somewhere along the journey, when the path starts to wind too much.

These elements are critical to all of your stakeholders, not just your employees. Without a clear vision of the results you are striving for and how you are going to get there, shareholders are forced to evaluate you solely on your current book value. Without an understanding or a feeling about your organizational purpose over and above your pursuit of profits, customers can only look at you transactionally. But on the other hand, when it is done right, you create a vision that enables employees to want to join the journey, customers to feel like they are a part of your company instead of just someone who gives you money, and shareholders to clearly understand how you are going to use their money for future growth and returns. That clarity attracts and binds these critical stakeholders together and harnesses that collective energy in a way that you could never do by force or will.

**Coaching Point: Your Vision is not for just for your employ-
ees - it should appeal to a broader consideration of your
network of stakeholders.**

■ TAKE AMAZON'S VISION AS AN EXAMPLE:

"To be Earth's most customer-centric company, where customers can
find and discover anything they might want to buy online, and en-
deavors to offer its customers the lowest possible prices."

In one sentence, Amazon lays out their What, Why and How, very
simply and cleanly:

- *What.* Amazon wants to be the place where shoppers go to
  buy anything online. Seems simple, but there is a tremendous
  amount packed into that simple statement. They do not segment
  out a portion of consumers – essentially everyone in the world is
  a potential customer. And clearly, they are not just in the book
  business any longer, like they were when they started. They want
  to sell anything you "might want to buy online". This profound-
  ly signals to shareholders that Amazon is a growth company, and
  that they are aiming at a huge market with a big payoff.

- *Why.* The source of passion at Amazon is the customer – "To be
  Earth's most customer-centric company". Again, they have set
  out a huge, global goal that would inspire anyone. But they have
  made it clear, if you are going to work at Amazon, you will have
  to have to be a fanatic about serving customer needs.

- *How.* They clearly believe that at least one way that they will be
  successful in attracting customers from all over the Earth to shop
  at Amazon for anything they might ever want to buy, is to offer
  the lowest possible prices. This communicates to customers that
  they should expect uncompromising value when they shop at
  Amazon, and challenges them to compare delivered price with
  any other retailer. They punctuate that point by actually allowing
  other retailers to sell on their site. Amazon doesn't care who ulti-

mately sells the product to the customer, as long as the customer gets the best value in the end.

So, in one statement, I know why I would invest in this company, work for this company, or buy from this company. . And in the case of this statement from Amazon, I call it bold, inspiring, and compelling organizational Vision.

In the next few chapters, we will explore each of the three questions that make up a great organizational Vision, and provide some frameworks and tools to help you answer those questions for your organization.

CHALK TALK

- To create a Vision for your organization, answer these key questions:

  > What is our destination and what does it look like?

  > Why should we bother taking the journey, and why do I, or anyone else, care?

  > How are we going to get from here to there, and how will we know if we have arrived?

- In addressing those key questions, make sure you consider the perspectives of Customers, Employees & Shareholders.

- When creating a Vision, ensure that it addresses the "Head, Heart and Hands" of your stakeholders

WHAT IS THE DESTINATION?

As I said, to most people, Dino Babers is not a household name, and when most people think of football, Syracuse is not the first thing that comes to mind. But the use of this example as a start to this book, and especially to this section that describes how to create a vision, strategy and culture for a team or an organization, was intentional. After all, most stories about how a great company or organization was built, start with a humble beginning – an inauspicious hero who overcomes great obstacles and goes on to achieve amazing things. In this story, that hero is you.

> *"As a leader, you can't just live in the present. You constantly have to think about the future as well[4]."*
>
> —Mike Shanahan,
> Head Coach, Denver Broncos

And one of the first steps you should take on your hero journey, is to decide upon your desired destination, your Vision for your organization. Remember this famous excerpt from the Cheshire Cat in the book, "Alice in Wonderland"?

. . . .
[4](Schefter & Shanahan, 1999)

"Alice: Would you tell me, please, which way I ought to go from here?

The Cheshire Cat: That depends a good deal on where you want to get to.

Alice: I don't much care where.

The Cheshire Cat: Then it doesn't much matter which way you go.

The cat punctuates a seemingly obvious point, in an unusual, pithy and powerful way. Simply put, be certain about where you are trying to go, before you begin the journey, because the destination will determine your path.

 Coaching Point: Your destination will determine your path. The order in which you define them is important -choosing your path before your destination can take you to a place you did not want to go.

Defining your desired future state is critical in any change initiative, and is at the center of any successful company or team. It creates the case for being; a reason why anyone would want to invest any incremental energy to be part of that enterprise or take part in that initiative. It creates an identity of who we want to be, and allows others to join us if they would like to share in that identity. Perhaps just as importantly, it helps those who don't share that vision to "get off the bus".

Choose Your Destination Carefully

Babers described his vision for the destination of his program through narrative, but as we discussed, you will not always have the time or opportunity to tell a long story to share your vision. Sooner or later, you will need to distill that vision down into a statement or phrase that will enable everyone to quickly see it for themselves. If he did, it might be something like,

"To deliver a fast-paced, aggressive style of football, that players want to play, and fans love to watch".

Organizations use these types of statements to engage their broad set of stakeholders in their vision. There are lots of examples from large enterprises that we can learn from. Here are just a few[5];

- Amazon—"To be earth's most customer-centric company; to build a place where people can come to find and discover anything they might want to buy online."

- J.C. Penny—"To be America's shopping destination for discovering great styles at compelling prices."

- CVS Caremark—"To improve the quality of human life."

- Kraft Foods—"To make today delicious."

- Toys 'R' Us—"To put joy in kids' hearts and a smile on parents' faces."

- Weyerhaeuser Company—"To release the potential in trees to solve important problems for people and the planet."

- Avon—"To be the company that best understands and satisfies the product, service, and self-fulfillment needs of women—globally."

Depending upon your perspective, these statements can seem aspirational and inspiring, or, utopian and somewhat flowery. Given the scope of the organizations represented above, an enterprise-wide vision is required to be somewhat broad.

When couched against the Amazon example, some might say that Babers' vision lacks the aspirational goal, or BHAG (Big Hairy Audacious Goal), that is often the trademark of corporate vision statements. He did not promise national championships. He did not promise that he would create Rhodes Scholars. He did not paint a picture of stu-

[5](Hull, 2012)

dent athletes visiting the kids in the children's hospital. So, while his teams may deliver all of those things, and I am sure Babers has expectations around all of those elements, they were not part of his core vision. And, I imagine that was likely intentional.

The Syracuse football program has a proud history[6]. During the 50's and 60's, under head coach Ben Schwartzwalder, the Orangemen were a perennial national power. In 1959, they won the national championship, capping the season by beating a dominant Texas Longhorn team in the Cotton Bowl, behind the running of Heisman Trophy winner, Ernie Davis. Again, during the 1990's, Syracuse had a very successful run, with a stretch of 11 bowl appearances over 14 seasons, winning 9 of them. But over the last several years, conference realignments have destabilized the program somewhat, recruiting has been a challenge, and the performance of the program has been sporadic, at best. So instead, Babers focused simply on the style of football he is going to bring to Syracuse, knowing that if he does that consistently, everything else is possible.

So, while many people might believe in the need of a BHAG to create inspiration, I am biased to creating visions that people can actually believe will come true, and in their lifetime. From my experience, once people believe a goal is either esoteric or utopian, they tend to disconnect their everyday behavior from it. And from my perspective, that devalues the entire purpose of actually having a coherent Vision in the first place.

 Coaching Point. Your Vision must be believable for anyone to meaningfully engage with it.

. . . .
[6](Various, Syracuse Orange Football, n.d.)

Consider Starbuck's vision for the company:

"Establish Starbucks as the premier purveyor of the finest coffee in the world while maintaining our uncompromising principles while we grow."

Very simple – be the top coffee shop without selling out on what we say matters to us. And that will be a significant challenge, because to be the best coffee shop in the world, they are going to have to sell top quality coffee and deliver it with amazing customer service. But Starbucks knows two things:

1. Coffee has a meaningful cost of goods and to maintain profitability, they are going to have to get their raw materials at a competitive cost. But at the same time, much of the world's best coffee is grown in developing nations. And as such, it would be easy for a large company like Starbucks to either drive down the quality of the product, or to negatively influence the treatment of the coffee growers to ensure their continued margin expansion. So, to uphold their vision, they will have to work creatively to concurrently ensure maximum coffee quality, while upholding fair trade practices to ensure they are encouraging sustainable farming and human rights practices.

2. Aside from the coffee beans, the next highest cost in a coffee shop is the labor. Again, given Starbuck's size, they hire a considerable number of people, and have an impact on the quality of life for their employees. To them, growing the business while negatively impacting these critical stakeholders, is not their vision of winning.

So, for Starbucks, their vision could be paraphrased as simply as "be a great, growing coffee shop, while positively impacting important stakeholders along the way". And if you patronize their business and/or read about their business you can see the results. They source their coffee beans responsibly, they support sensible farming practices, and they pay above average wages, provide medical benefits, and support employees further their education. It is a powerful, yet simple and attainable vision. Not easy to execute I am sure, but one that is visibly attainable, and something that can inspire their employees, customers and supply chain partners, every day.

 Coaching Point: Clearly communicate what winning means, and doesn't mean, in your Vision statements.

Communicate Your Destination Viscerally

Let's revisit Baber's vision of his desired future state of Syracuse football:

> *"You are in the Carrier Dome. The house is filled. The feeling is electric. The noise is deafening. You have a defense that is relentless. You have a special teams which has been well-coached. You have an offense that will not huddle. And you have a game that is faster than you have ever seen on turf. Open your eyes. That is going to be a reality. That is going to be Syracuse football. Thank you"*

In that one minute, Babers described, very viscerally, his vision for the Syracuse Orangemen football program. Moreover, he didn't rely only on his words to share his vision. He very deliberately had everyone close their eyes to transport themselves to the Syracuse home stadium, the Carrier Dome, and imagine themselves at a game, taking part in that vision. He described how it would look ("filled"), how it would feel ("electric"), and how it would sound ("deafening"). In doing so he brought that vision to life, making it palpably real for everyone in the audience.

Coca-Cola also does this well. Consider their vision for the company and the brand:

> *"To refresh the world…To inspire moments of optimism and happiness"*

When you say the phrase, you can almost hear the top coming off of a can or a bottle, and see the joy on someone's face as they "Enjoy Coca-Cola". In doing so, they viscerally create the feeling of "happiness" which is their vision.

Have a Vivid Imagination

Babers and Coca-Cola are harnessing the power of the human imagination. It is a scientifically proven fact that the mind cannot tell the difference between something that has been vividly imagined, and reality. So, the more vivid and visceral you can make your vision, the more real it will be for your stakeholders, and the higher likelihood that they fully engage with it.

 Coaching Point: When you create your vision, use your imagination and try to leverage all of your senses - how it will look, what you will hear people say, the way it will make you feel.

Dino Babers painted a very clear picture to describe his intended destination, his desired future state. His description allows anyone, not just an insider or statistician, to know what that future state looks like, so they will recognize it when they are living it. And he carefully chose a destination that is real, and attainable for his organization, and one that people are going to immediately be able to attach themselves to, and believe in.

CHALK TALK
WHAT IS THE DESIRED FUTURE STATE?

- A vivid Imagination allows people to see your desired destination and that makes it real

- Use powerful visual and sensory imagery – don't just describe what it looks like, make people feel what it will be like

- Identify tangible, observable signs to success –let people recognize it when they see it happening

- Ensure that it can be real and attainable – a vision must be executable, or it is simply daydreaming

WHY SHOULD I CARE?

Nick Saban, is the head coach of the Alabama Crimson Tide, a storied program in the history of college football. Bear Bryant coached Alabama to multiple national championships, and is often considered one of the best, if not the best, college football coach of all time. But under Saban, Alabama has delivered a level of sustained success greater than Bryant ever achieved. His program is at the pinnacle of the sport, and can easily be referred to as a dynasty.

He is noted for his focus on execution, but Saban credits a compelling vision with the success of his teams. He is quoted as saying, "First of all, you have to have a vision that answers the question, "What kind of a program do I want to have?". But then, just as importantly, you have to "get people to buy into it[7]." And "buying into it" means adhering to the vision when the going gets rough.

Provide a Purpose

His core belief is that creating a vision is easy, but that the difficult thing is having people truly buy into it, to have the perseverance to do the things necessary, and to do them consistently, to fulfill the

[7](Cases, 2015)

vision. For college football players, that is getting into the weight room before your early morning classes, making the comprehensive nutritional sacrifices part of your everyday routine, and spending long hours in the film room studying your upcoming opponent, on top of scheduled practices and a full academic schedule. For business leaders, it means investing the time to develop your people while still delivering on your own contribution accountabilities, spending time out with customers while balancing time with family, and building customer relationships while still executing your operational and administrative responsibilities.

Success on the football field is the output of many months and years of arduous work. Success in business is difficult, and requires sacrifice. That is what makes winning sweet. But it is the power of the vision that makes the struggle possible. It is why we get up in the morning and put in the hard work that makes success possible. To sustain people through that struggle, it has to mean more to them than just winning the game or hitting a quarterly number. It must give them purpose.

A purpose is critical to sustainable success, because it reaches people on a personal and emotional level, and galvanizes their commitment to the organization in a way that transcends the attachment that comes from winning results in the short term. It clarifies for everyone individually, why they come to work each day, and fuels their ability to give extraordinary effort in pursuit of goals. It is often what separates "one hit wonders" from an organization that delivers above average shareholder returns, or championships, over extended periods of time.

 Coaching Point: A purpose can fuel engagement during the ordinary or difficult execution of the business, and can inspire stakeholders during uninspiring times.

In their powerful book, "It is Not What You Sell, It is What You Stand For"[8], authors Roy Spence and Haley Rushing detail the power that Purpose can deliver to an organization. Spence is one of the founders of the advertising agency, GSD&M in Austin, and Rushing is the Chief Purposologist and co-founder of The Purpose Institute. During their time building winning brands, including Walmart, Southwest Airlines, John Deere, Whole Foods Market and BMW, they refocused their branding to support the Purpose of the organization, to amazing success

When it is authentic, it transforms a strategy into a movement. It changes Southwest's "Low Fares Everyday" to "Giving You the Freedom to Fly". It allows for your key stakeholders to care not only for what you are doing, but also why you are doing it. When Southwest began as a business in the late 60's, a relatively small percentage of the people in the U.S. flew regularly.

"When I started working on Southwest Airlines, I kid you not, only people flying on business, and the very wealthy people, ever flew."

—Herb Kelleher, CEO, Southwest Airlines, retired

So, by operating the business leanly, using only one kind of plane, and turning flights faster, they were able to offer lower fares than the typical "hub and spoke" airlines. In so doing, they were making air travel more accessible to more people, thus "democratizing the skies". In that story, the customer is the "hero", who uses that new freedom to fly, to explore new places, and to visit with family and friends who are far away. Southwest Airlines has consistently been rated one of the "most admired companies", and their success at bringing their purpose to life is a big reason why.

[8](Spence & Rushing)

To be more than the initiative "du jour", a purpose must have two mutually reinforcing attributes; it must engage the passions of the organization's comprehensive set of stakeholders, and it must be aligned to the business results the organization pursues on a daily basis. In most cases, that means delivering a profit, while also delivering some value for society or the world. If either of these elements is weak or unclear, the purpose will either fail to gather the necessary critical mass, or will not feel genuine. Either way, it will fizzle out, and likely damage the organizational culture, and impair organizational leadership credibility.

 Coaching Point: To be sustainable, your purpose must be directly correlated to the everyday operations of your business. If not, it will end up being perceived as simple philanthropy. That is respectable, but it often does not create the intangible draw that a purpose can.

When these two things are in balance, you have a chance to build a business that is sustainable – one that will stand the test of time. If your target purpose is separate or tangential from your core business, your people will never be able to stay focused and passionate about it.

Connecting to all stakeholders

When Mack Brown joined The University of Texas in 1997, it was a program that was steeped with history and pageantry, but one that had fallen into a period of mediocrity. The key stakeholders around The University remembered well the twenty years under Darrell Royal that included consistent conference championships, and several national championships. Brown's vision could be nothing less. However, the current state of the program was considerably different from that picture of success. As such, he was going to need considerable resources, and a significant effort from a lot of people. He was going to need more than just a check, he was going to need their heart and soul.

One of the reasons for the lack of success was the failure of the past three coaches, and especially his predecessor, to make meaningful relationships with the people in and around the program that mattered most; donors, influential alumni, potential recruits, high school football coaches, university leaders, and even the fan base. Understanding this, Brown painstakingly met with his wide array of important stakeholders, and listened carefully to what they needed, and expected from the football program (more about Coach Brown's approach to stakeholder management later). Upon careful reflection of what he found, he crafted the Purpose of the program; to "Win Championships with Good Kids that Graduate". While it does not have the philanthropic feel of Walmart's purpose of helping people to "Save Money and Live Better", it is specific and descriptive relative to a higher purpose, and it engages the broad set of stakeholders that Brown had to manage as the head coach.

If we go back to our first section on creating a Vision, he fulfilled the key tenets of a powerful vision. Everyone can imagine what winning championships with good kids who graduate looks like. You can clearly visualize the championship post-game press conferences, the Twitter posts of players graduating, and the warm family environment pictures on Facebook. It sparks the imagination, the vision is vivid, and it is not at all fantastical – it is something that all his stakeholders believe can become a reality.

While a few fans might be satisfied with just "Win Championships", Coach Brown was not. His personal beliefs would never allow him to lead a program that wins with players of low character, who were recruited improperly, who didn't really participate academically, or who would not represent the university in a way that the university and its alumni could be proud of. And moreover, most of his stakeholders shared one or all of those motivations. Brown knew that winning championships, doing it the right way, and with integrity to the words, were not mutually exclusive. This was a purpose that resonated with the passions of not only himself, but of the people that would decide his fate within his dream job.

 Coaching Point: Know your stakeholders and what their purposes are. If your vision is at odds with that purpose, soon enough, that stakeholder will be at odds with you.

For Brown to be successful with "Winning Championships with Good Kids who Graduate", he was going to need a certain kind of player. And while most talented high school athletes would be inclined to tell a coach that they were a "good kid", and were focused on graduating, as well as playing football at a high level, how would Brown know which ones truly were? Here is one benefit of stating your Purpose definitively. His clear declaration of Purpose did a lot of the work for him. It clearly communicated to all the recruits that if you fancied yourself as a bit of a "bad boy", or if you weren't really interested in going to class, that maybe Texas wasn't right for you. That message would reach not only players, but their families and high school coaches as well. And once he had relationships built up with local high school coaches, they would help identify the players that would be a good fit for his program.

But communicating his Purpose spoke to a broader set of stakeholders than just recruits. It clearly spoke to, and served the Athletic department's Purpose of Winning with Integrity. So, they knew what they could expect from Brown with respect to recruiting properly, and bringing in kids that would represent the school in a positive way.

It also informed the academic leaders within the university that Brown would not be stretching the boundaries of academic integrity, and would expect his players to be making progress towards a degree. By the end of his tenure, the Longhorn football program had one of the strongest graduation records among peer universities.

Coaching Point: Your purpose signals to your stakeholders what you stand for, and helps you attract people that believe in your Vision, and filter out the people that do not.

Finally, it set clear expectations with alumni and fans of the program. Brown clearly stated that his expected level of performance there at Texas was "winning championships". In the twenty years that had passed since Coach Darrell Royal had left Texas, championships were rare. But Texas fans remembered the "good old days", and expected the program to perform at an elite level. So, while he had yet to prove it on the field, Brown had taken an important first step by letting his fan base know that championships were again to be considered the bar of success at the University of Texas. Brown's clear design for the Purpose of the football program fundamentally changed the school's relationship to its stakeholders as evidenced by clear changes in behavior.

It began with the fans. Long a laissez faire crowd that often arrived late in the first quarter, and perhaps more concerned with the pre-game tailgate, burnt orange fans came out in droves. Season tickets nearly doubled during his time at Texas.

Donors jumped on board as well[9]. Donations to the Athletic department skyrocketed during Brown's time at Texas, financing stadium expansions, infrastructure improvements, and the most amazing athletic facilities ever seen.

Top recruits in the state of Texas noticed too, and now lined up for Texas after years of leaving the state for other programs. Brown set a pace that other programs could not match, and that had not been seen before in college football. Often, Brown would have his recruiting class completely signed up a full year in advance, before his peers had even gotten started.

. . . .
[9](Karp, 2009)

Coaching Point: A Vision allows people to see your destination. A Purpose will make them take action on behalf of it.

Brown even managed to make inroads with the academic community at UT. Long-simmering animosity between the academic faculty and the athletic department, fueled by a perception of misplaced priorities for an institution of higher learning, were significantly improved under Brown. His clear focus on "kids who graduate", backed up by strong academic progress statistics by the football program were major contributors. But, Brown's success in raising revenue, and sharing that success with the Physics department didn't hurt either. In unprecedented move for college athletics, UT's athletic used some of its revenue to fund academic endowments. Athletics is generally a cost center supported by the general fund, not the other way around.

So, in summary, while many current philosophies focus heavily on one type of stakeholder, Brown's success could be attributed to his ability to see into the hearts of his full set of stakeholders. He took the time to understand their particular passions, and ensured that the organizational purpose in support of helping him reach the destination identified in his Vision.

Mapping out your stakeholders

Stakeholder	Their importance to the organization	Their passion towards the purpose
The University	The ultimate authority over the program came from the school, of course	The program should reflect well on the University as a place of higher learning and academic integrity
The Athletic Department	The athletic director was Brown's boss, and makes decision around funding of initiatives	Their stated purpose is "Winning with Integrity", so they are focused on athletic achievement while the maintaining ethical standards of the University

Alumni	They are fans of the team who ultimately consume the product on the field and fund the operations of the department	They want to see a winning program that they are proud of, and to enjoy the camaraderie and emotional attachment to the team and the university
Recruits/Players	They are the talent of the organization, and they need to be inspired to choose the University of Texas, to give incremental effort both on the field and in the classroom, and to behave in a way consistent with being a "nice kid"	They want to play at a prestigious institution where they can win championships, and they and their families need to believe that the program cares about them enough to ensure they are getting an education as well
High School Coaches	They are the talent "brokers" for the organization, whose affiliation and trust in the University is critical, to ensure that they will recommend the school to their very best players who trust their opinion and guidance	They want to be seen as a valued partner to the University, and someone that is valued as a successful teacher and mentor to the young men that are recruited
Prominent Donors	They provide the capital budget that funds stadium expansions, new facilities, and any capital-intensive requirements	They want special access to the team and University, and want to believe that their support is a major factor in the on-field success of the team

FIGURE 2. STAKEHOLDER MAP FOR MACK BROWN

Brown was able to translate that Purpose for the program into results, both on the field and off[10]. Coach Brown delivered UT's first national championship in 35 years, during a ten-year run of at least 10 wins, returning the Longhorns to college football royalty – a position established during the Darrell Royal era. Inspired by this success, ESPN created the "Longhorn Network", a 24 hour channel focused solely on Longhorn Sports, a first in the industry, and a testament to the strength of the UT brand. The renewed enthusiasm in the program brought increased ticket, concession and licensing revenue, catapulting Texas to the top earning program in the country. Brown more than doubled the athletic budget for the program during his tenure. And while Coach Brown resigned after the 2013 season, he retired as one of the winningest coaches in college football history, his tenure will be considered a golden era for Longhorn football – one that reshaped the program for decades to come.

But, how does this play out in the world of business? I have consulted with many purpose-driven companies over the years, and have seen the amazing impact that a well-crafted, and well-executed purpose can have. Let's explore how Walmart aligns its key stakeholders by communicating and driving their Purpose, "Save More, Live Better", as opposed to their old tagline of "Low Prices, Every Day".

Crafting a purpose that engages your stakeholders

Walmart is a large enterprise; that is owned by millions of shareholders, that generates over $400B in revenue, that is served by thousands of suppliers, that is driven by over 2 million Associates (employees), that has over 11,000 stores worldwide, and where 100 million people shop at every week. As such, they have one of the largest stakeholder networks of any company. So, how they engage these stakeholders has a material effect on the sustainability of the organization.

....

[10](Rishe, 2013)

By communicating a clear purpose, they change the nature of the conversation they have with their stakeholders.

Stakeholder	Before	After
Customers	We want to save you money	We want you to live a better life, and we help you do that by allowing to afford more
Employees	We need to control our costs	We are here to make our customers' lives better, and the costs we save, we pass on to our customers
Suppliers	We need you to lower your prices	Join us in helping our customers live better. We will pass the savings you provide to us, on to them
Shareholders	We will deliver a great profit next quarter	We will provide a sustainable return well into the future

FIGURE 3. WALMART'S PURPOSE TO THEIR STAKEHOLDERS

So, you might be wondering, "so, if I engage my people in our noble purpose, will they will truly behave differently, and that will that create differentiated results?" While this concept may sound a bit utopian, it is supported by research, as well as by pure common sense. In their seminal work, "The Service Profit Chain[11]", Heskett, Sasser, and Schlesinger clarify the connection between companies inspiring their people, and those employees taking care of customers; creating loyalty, revenue and profit growth.

Connecting Employees to Customers

In a follow up article, "Putting the Service Profit Chain to Work"[12], they discuss the concept of the 'internal quality of the workplace", as a key

....
[11](Heskett, Sasser, & Schlesinger, 1997)
[12](Heskett, Schlesinger, Sasser, Jones, & Loveman, 2008)

driver of employee satisfaction. They describe that it is measured by the employees' feelings to their jobs, customers, colleagues and their companies. Their research points to employees' belief in their ability to create results for customers as the primary driver of that perception of internal quality.

One of the companies they researched was the insurance company, USAA. USAA's Purpose, "We know what it means to serve", is at the heart of this connection between employees and customers. USAA focuses primarily on "serving" veterans, who have "served" in the military. By operationalizing their Purpose, and creating a virtuous circle of serving those who have served our country, they have transformed a business strategy into a noble pursuit. And when that intent is genuine, it can have startling results. USAA continuously tops the charts in customer satisfactions ratings, which has translated to industry-leading customer and employee retention.

To create a winning football program, coaches must create a "purpose" that players inspires their players. Simply winning games is not enough to sustain an entire team of players through a difficult season that may include pain and injury. Large enterprises have the same challenge, but their "game" goes on every day – day after day. Suffice it to say, that creating, communicating, and fostering a Purpose that excites, impassions, and incites employees to engage with customers in a deeper, more authentic way, is critical to sustainable success. It is just another example of a business lesson that we can take from the world of football.

CHALK TALK
DEFINING THE PURPOSE OF YOUR ORGANIZATION

Your Purpose Should:	Ask Yourself:
Be powerful and inspiring	Is your purpose compelling?
	Can it turn your business into a passionate pursuit?
Be relevant to the business you are in, and create tangible impact	Is your Purpose is central to your company's core business?
	Can your company truly deliver impact on the Purpose?
	Does your purpose connect how your business makes money to how it serves the planet or our fellow man?
Address the needs of all of your stakeholders	Have you considered the needs of shareholders, employees, and customers at the minimum, and at best, include suppliers and the communities that the organization serves?
	Can your stakeholders answer the "What's In It For Me?" question (WIIFM)?
Meaningfully Connect Employees to Customers	Must deeply understand the connection between how your employees and customers, and how their loyalty turns into growth and profitability

HOW DO WE GET THERE?

When Mack Brown set out his vision for the football program at The University of Texas, by communicating that it would "Win championships with good kids that graduate", he laid a very clear picture of what success looked like. It was written in language that everyone could understand and picture in their head, it was inspiring, and it spoke to all of the stakeholders to whom he was responsible. But, to be effective, it must provide something else – clarity on how the program is going to get there. It should define guidelines for everyone on how to behave, and show how to easily and objectively measure success.

Thomas Edison once said that "Ideas without execution, are hallucinations". And nothing frustrates enterprise business stakeholders, or football fans, more, than thinking that their appointed leaders are hallucinating when they communicate their vision and goals. Having a clear path forward makes your vision palpable, and makes it easy for your stakeholders to buy into it. That path forward will be defined by two simple concepts; setting clear and measurable goals that define the destination, and an honest assessment of your current state that will quantify the gap between where you are and where you are going.

Setting Clear Objective Goals

We discussed the importance of carefully balancing a vision that captures the imagination of your stakeholders, while not being so far reaching that it feels...imaginary. So, that step – setting clear goals, with objective methods of determining whether the vision was reached or not, is paramount.

For Mack Brown, with his vision of "Win Championships With Good Kids Who Graduate", he established objective goals, that were simple and measurable;

- **Win Championships....** During the bulk of Brown's tenure at Texas, he was in a conference with elite programs like Oklahoma and Nebraska, who were consistently ranked as the top programs in the country. So, for Brown, "winning championships", simply winning his conference was going to be a significant goal. While his ultimate goal was clearly winning national championships, he was pragmatic enough to recognize that in the 100 years of college football, very few programs had won back-to-back championships, and that even a program as storied as The University of Texas, there had only been 3 national championships in its history. So, if he chose the national championship as his goal, it might be taken as unrealistic by some, and at the very least, most years would be considered a failure. Moreover, since the Big 12 was so well-respected, winning the conference title would nearly always put you in the mix for the national championship game, and losing it would almost certainly eliminate you from that opportunity. So, every year, his goal was the same - to simply to win the Big 12 Championship. That kept the players grounded, and focused on the game in front of them, since every conference game was critical. The ultimate beauty of this goal is that it never changed. So his metric here was clear – win the Big 12, every year.

- **...With Good Kids...** While this could certainly be perceived as the vaguest of the goals in his vision, measurement by his most important stakeholders was simple, and therefore, it was quite clear. Sadly enough, one of the most troubling, and voyeuristic elements of college football, is watching a college student athlete act like anything but that. While I will address this in greater detail when we discuss Culture, for now, sadly, a "good kid", is simply a kid not being a "bad kid". And what defines a "bad kid"? In this case, as in most cases, your stakeholders – customers, investors, employees, the community at large – decide what is good and bad, regardless of what you think. And as your stakeholders, they are the arbiter of both that classification, and what should be done about it. Brown's stakeholders simply did not want to hear stories about kids doing "bad things". Without going into all of the sensationalistic stories about what constitutes "bad things", we can agree that we all know what those things are. So, for Brown, his goal of winning with good kids was simple – win games without having players show up on the police blotter, or making news for things other than success on the football field, in the classroom, and out in the community. So, his metric here was also clear – no publicly negative incidents from players, every year.

- **...Who Graduate.** While many people today scoff, and use the description "student athlete", sarcastically. Brown did not see it that way. Historically, statistics have shown that college student athletes have graduated at a higher rate than that of the general university student population, and Brown expected that at Texas. Due to the overall success of his program financially, he was able to fund all of the academic support that he needed to ensure that his athletes had every chance to be successful in the classroom, as well as on the field. Now that is not to minimize the challenges that athletes at a football program as competitive as Texas, will face in maintaining focus on academics. The time commitment is significant, and the temptations outside the classroom and locker room are also significant for 18-21 year old men. Moreover, many of Brown's players will have the opportunity to leave school early for professional athletic careers, so they may not even stay long enough to achieve a degree on the first pass (though many of his past athletes have returned to school to finish their degree once established in, or retired from, the NFL). But, many peer programs were having difficulty with their academic performance, so the NCAA stepped in and created a metric and a comprehensive measurement approach. So, his metric was again clear – have a graduation rate that met the expectations of the NCAA, and the president of the University of Texas – his two primary stakeholders in this area, every year.

So, in this way, Mack Brown was able to communicate a Vision that outlined clear success metrics, and made it transparent to everyone whether he was succeeding or not. Brown's success in his football program was significant in all three areas, and one of his keys to success was by setting clear goals and metrics with his key stakeholders. And by having them be consistent year after year, he enabled the program to focus on the same goals, and to simply refine the tactics to reach them each year.

Amazon provides an interesting case example for setting clear goals to support an organizational vision. From 2006 to 2013, Marc Onetto served as the SVP of Worldwide Operations and Customer Service. So, clearly, Onetto's organization had a huge role in ensuring that Amazon's vision of being "Earth's most customer-centric company" was real. He was responsible for all aspects of supply chain and delivery, as well as holistic view of the customer experience. So, to fulfill the promise of customer centricity, he knew he had to get shipments there quick, and for the lowest possible cost. And since they are committed to being the best in the world at this, he shared his vision for Amazon's customer service as being "to deliver everything, at the very moment a customer determines they need it (and not a second earlier or later), with no packaging[13]." At first read, that may seem to fit the definition of unrealistic that I mentioned earlier, but if you are a customer of Amazon, or just attuned to the business world at all, I am sure you have realized that this is not a fantasy. Amazon is making meaningful strides towards that vision every day. Amazon is relentless – relentless in looking for ways to trim one second out of every step in the fulfillment process, relentless in looking for new ways to overcome bottlenecks in the supply chain – even exploring the idea of using drones, and relentless in their focus on advocating for the customer at every turn.

But every period, they set clear goals of the level of performance they want to get to, and that are easily measurable. They combined an inspiring vision with clear goals that make the vision easy to buy into, and simple to know whether or not you succeeding in achieving it.

 Coaching Point: Choose goals that are easily measurable, and when possible, plainly visible to your stakeholders without arduous computation.

Clarifying the Current State

But before Amazon can create a plan to reach their delivery performance and customer experience metric goals for the Desired Future State, you first must have an honest accounting of the Current State. Your constituents are going to do that immediately, either publicly or privately. As soon as you begin painting the vivid picture of your imagined Future State, your stakeholders will be taking stock of the Current State, to determine whether what you are describing is fantasy, or a possible reality. So, for you to be successful in laying out the path forward, you must first realistically assess your current situation relative to your Vision. As an analogy from today's tech-

. . . .

[13](Onetto, 2009)

nology, the mapping function on your phone or PC can lay out a path to anywhere on Earth, but you must first tell the application your starting position.

That honest assessment is important, as it quantifies the size of the gap between your Desired Future State and the Current State. It clarifies the magnitude of the journey you are embarking on; a journey you are asking your stakeholders to take with you. In many cases, it is easy to describe, as it is often in contrast to the destination. In Babers' example, one can easily imagine the current state in light of his description of the desired future state:

Described Element	Desired Future State	Implied Current State
Attendance	"stadium is filled"	Attendance way below capacity
Fan Noise Level	"deafening"	Quiet or unenthusiastic
Stadium Atmosphere	"electric"	Apathetic
Special Teams performance	"well-coached"	Undisciplined, prone to mistakes
Defense	"relentless"	Yielding as the game wears on
Offense	"no huddle"	Plodding
Team Speed	"fastest you have ever seen"	underwhelming

FIGURE 4. HOW A DESIRED FUTURE STATE IMPLIES A CURRENT STATE

Any leader tasked with turning around a team or organization must be able to create a clear contrast to the past or Current State. In many cases, if you are brought in to lead an organization, it is because the past leader was unsuccessful. On the other hand, it is often not healthy to paint the current situation with too much of a negative brush. After all, no one wants to look at themselves too negatively, or to hear "their baby being called ugly". But suffice it to say, the best approach is to describe the Current State honestly and fairly, noting what things are solid and working, as much as what is not. When possible, use measurable statistics. For Babers, that might include attendance records, kick coverage statistics, and the number of offensive plays executed per game. In so doing, he has the ability to couch those current statistics against his known targets, or at the very least forecasted improvements.

Using data and clear metrics to describe a corporate vision is just as important, because businesses keep score as well. They were critical to the success of Robert Nardelli's Vision that he established for Home Depot when he took over in 2000[14]. Home Depot was in the middle of an historic performance run, reaching $40B in sales faster than any retailer in history. But the weight of their growing scale, and the emergence of a serious competitor in Lowe's was challenging their continued success. They achieved this growth with an entrepreneurial, customer service focused culture. However, that culture was not grounded in operational discipline, and that lack of discipline was inflating the required working capital, limiting inventory turns, and negatively impacting profitability.

Nardelli, an ex-GE executive, was the right person for this job. He described the Desired Future State, which was a fundamentally sound operating model with a more methodical approach to merchandising and a well-organized supply chain. As such, while the picture of success – a more disciplined operational environment – wasn't inspiring. Hopefully, the vividness of the benefits – improved earnings that translated to a higher stock price and bigger employee bonuses - that would come along with it, made it a reality worth pursuing.

. . . .

[14](Charan, 2006)

However, unlike Babers, Nardelli wasn't inheriting a losing team, and whose stakeholders could clearly see the problems in the organization. As aforementioned, Home Depot was growing rapidly, and its stock price reflected that success, increasing roughly 50% in 1999 and splitting 3 shares for 2 at the end of the year.

So, with the "scoreboard" clearly in your favor, how do you create any urgency to change, and convince the "team" that there are serious improvements that need to be made? You use data. He carefully laid out the Current State of all of their key operating metrics, and supported those metrics with actual customer feedback on where operational issues were impacting their experience. Punctuating the Current State data with actual customer comments was critical and intentional, as Home Depot's Purpose – the source of passion for employees – was rooted in helping customers. After all, their slogan around this period had been "You Can Do This. We Can Help."

So, in this case, Nardelli showed a picture of the future that was punctuated improved financial performance that would create value for shareholders and employees. But unlike most leadership changes on football teams that are necessitated by past poor performance, he was challenged to create urgency to change due to the success the organization was currently experiencing. So, using data to clarify the Current state became critical.

Hall of Fame football coach, Bill Parcells, is often quoted as saying, "You are what your record says you are". It speaks to the challenges leaders have in creating accountability in organizations. You hear the disconnect in everyday language in business – "we are a great company. We have just had below average earnings the last few years." You hear the same types of issues in everyday life as well – "he is a good person. He just does bad things." Parcells would disagree. If you are delivering below average earnings, you are a below average company. If you are a guy who does bad things, you are a bad guy. That honest assessment of your Current State will help clarify where you are relative to your destination, and build the urgency you need to get the organization to move.

 Coaching Point: You are what your record says you are. Honestly quantify your current performance to establish where you are, relative to your destination.

Clarifying the Gap

By measuring the difference between the Current State and the Desired State, you provide yourself with several important insights. You have defined what success looks like in tangible terms, and you have quantified where you stand today. The size or nature of the gap between your current and future states will help you identify the type of strategy that will be required to close it. Does the job call for pruning shears, or a chainsaw? Are you sweeping up dust, or are you moving boulders? That can help you better understand what types of resources or budget you are going to need to realistically bring your vision to reality. It is critical for you to get alignment on your resource requirements from your key stakeholders, before sharing your vision for the organization. There is no point in trying to paint a picture of the future, if you can't afford paint. If it is a bold vision worth pursuing, you will likely not be able to bring your vision to life alone, and it will likely require resources beyond your own.

Clarifying the gap will also shed light on the approach you will need to take to close it. Does your Vision require an entirely new direction, or is it more about doing the same things better? For people to engage in your vision for the future, they have to have a basic understanding of what the journey will look like. As an example, for Babers, he made his approach relatively clear; he was going to install an entirely new offensive system. That system was comprised of a completely new operating language, a new style of playing the game that would require a different set of skills, and certainly, and new personnel that had those skills. And in college football, you can only acquire new talent once per year. And since the college athletics experience is based on a four-year period of eligibility, you turn over about 25% of your talent each year. Obviously, in the world of business, especially large enterprise, your ability to transform your talent can take much longer.

For Nardelli, it was not about installing a new offensive philosophy, it was about installing a new culture[15]. The entrepreneurial working environment that had so successfully driven Home Depot through the rapid growth phase, was the underlying issue that was impeding their operational efficiency and strangling their cash flow. For Nardelli, it was clear, "What so effectively got Home Depot from zero to $50 billion in sales, wasn't going to get it to the next $50 billion."

But again, given the success of the company, many employees did not see the need to change. They had no interest in some outsider coming into their company, and "GE-izing" their customer-focused, entrepreneurial culture. So, instead of changing a lot of policies at the outset, what he introduced was transparency. He made all of the key operational metrics for all functions, regions and stores open and available to everyone. In this way, he was able to clearly establish what the performance gaps in the company were, and what was working, and what was not. It allowed his leadership team to see for themselves the gaps that needed to be addressed, and to take ownership for the resolution.

Understanding the time horizon required to realistically reach your Desired Future State is critical to your success. One of the most important pieces of your communication to providing guidance as to what stakeholders expect, and when, with respect to the results you are promising in that new future. Setting unrealistic, or unclear, expectations for stakeholders, is the primary reason many leaders do

[15](Charan, 2006)

not get to stay in their positions long enough to see their Desired Future State realized. For Babers, his promised change was not national championships, or even conference championships. He sold a vision of a style of play; one that would be exciting and fun to watch. He knew that most of his stakeholders that were listening would believe that one would lead to the other, but he was careful not to promise that.

His challenge at Syracuse was more immediate than Nardelli was experiencing at Home Depot. His most pressing challenge was to drive engagement; with alumni donors, ticket buying fans, and recruits. Without that engagement, he could lose the faith of his stakeholders relatively quickly, and derail any possibility for success in the future. As such his description of this Desired Future State needed to be more reachable in the short term. So, he provided visual indicators that were likely to be visible right away – ensuring some short-term wins that would begin to drive belief in his initiative. For business leaders the need is the same, and the stakes are just as high. Your vision for the organization should include not only a vivid, palpable description of the future, but also clarity as to what stakeholders should expect and when.

 Coaching Point: Understand your time horizon. Your stakeholders define how long of a journey they are willing to go on with you before they can start seeing signs of your defined destination.

Finally, you need to answer a very important question about your Desired Future State –Why Now? What current circumstances exist that make it imperative that your team or organization embark on this journey, now? Any meaningful vision of the future is going to take some effort, and change is often caustic. Things could get worse before they get better. Why should people run to this pain, at this particular time? We all have to pay taxes, but paying them later is always better. Why should we do it NOW? To help you create the level of urgency you need, try looking at that question from the opposite direction. What would happen if we did nothing, or simply chose to pursue this initiative at some time in the future?

For Babers, this was a powerful tool at his disposal. With Syracuse now in a "Power 5" conference, the payoff for success is higher. Power 5 conferences have access to bigger television contracts, and a more direct path to the top bowl games and the national championship. So, the "Why Now" question was impactful. Moreover, now that they were in an elite football conference, the level of competition they would be facing on a regular basis would be increasingly tougher. And they would have to face them without being located in an area known as a recruiting hotbed. They would need to upgrade their talent to be successful, and would not be successful at doing that without a clear, exciting Vision to sell. Without that, they would quickly fall behind the competition, creating a larger and larger Gap to overcome. So, the "What if we Don't?" question was valuable as well.

 Coaching Point: Create urgency to close the gap by helping your stakeholders see the implications of NOT taking action.

Nardelli used both of these questions to his advantage as well. He developed urgency by making operational data visible to his employees, and demonstrating where they were underperforming relative to the competition, and even in the eyes of the customer. And by using that same data, he was able to communicate how amazing the Desired State would be, and why it was worth the journey.

CHALK TALK
CLARIFYING & CLOSING THE GAP

Accepted Current State	The Gap	Desired Future State
• Not overly pessimistic, but clearly differentiated from the Future State	• Quantify the Size and/or Clarify the Nature	• Clear goals that are reasonable to stakeholders
• Validates what is solid/working	• Type & Amount of Resources Required to Close it	• Tangible evidence of success; we will know when we are living it
• Rooted in accepted metrics	• Approach to Closing it; New direction, or just more/better	
• Honors the elements of the organization that support the Purpose	• How long until we see some results? What can we expect, when?	• Realistic & Attainable
	• Why Now? What if we Don't Close the Gap?	• Appeals to all Stakeholders

**FIGURE 5. CLARIFYING THE GAP BETWEEN
CURRENT AND FUTURE STATE**

Summary

Great leaders and organizations are often defined by the inspiring and ambitious visions they set. They are inspiring, because they capture the imaginations of their stakeholders by vividly describing the destination defined by that Vision, like the one Dino Babers shared for Syracuse University and Howard Schultz created for Starbucks. The get those stakeholders to emotionally invest in that Vision by instilling it with a Purpose above and beyond wins and losses, or dollars and cents like Mack Brown did at The University of Texas and Herb Kelleher did at Southwest Airlines. And the honestly lay out the challenge in front of the organization by frankly addressing the current reality like Bill Parcells and Robert Nardelli at Home Depot. When those three elements are addressed properly, an organizational Vision can drive amazing results. Bill Parcells led several successful franchises and the New York football Giants to two Super Bowl titles[16]. Mack Brown led the Longhorns through a dynastic run of 10 consecutive years of at least 10 wins and a national championship. And as of this writing, in 2017, Babers' Syracuse Orangemen defeated the reigning national champion, Clemson, in what will likely not be his last major victory. Few would argue with the success that Amazon, Starbucks, Southwest Airlines and Home Depot have realized in the marketplace as they are each the leader in their industry category.

In this section, we have discussed how fundamentally sound organizations have clear visions that inspire stakeholders and guide the behaviors and decisions toward its goals. A clear and compelling vision must answer three important questions for stakeholders:

- *What is our destination?* The Vision must paint a vivid picture of the future state of the organization; one that captures the imagination of all of its stakeholders. The clearer the Vision, the more likely that people will capture their imagination, and help them believe it can become a reality.

- *Why do I care?* That Vision must be inspirational to the stakeholders over and above the day-to-day grind that enables everyone to earn their daily bread. It should be something that gives all stakeholders a higher purpose, instilling a sense of pride and emotional bond to the organization and the work.

- *How do we get there?* The Vision should be supported by clear goals, that people can see, and ones that they feel are realistic and attainable. As a leader, it is your job to honestly assess and communicate the organization's current performance, and the

. . . .
[16](Various, Bill Parcells, n.d.)

gap that exists between the Current State and the Desired Future State. That honesty will form the basis of the organization's communication between stakeholders, transforming finger-pointing into collaborative feedback to a shared goal.

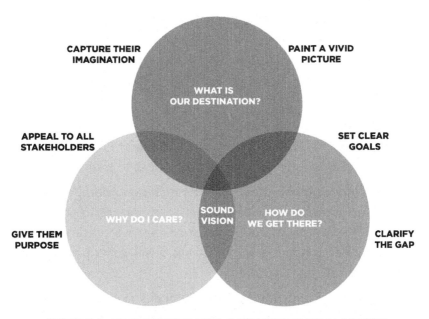

CAPTURE THEIR IMAGINATION

PAINT A VIVID PICTURE

WHAT IS OUR DESTINATION?

APPEAL TO ALL STAKEHOLDERS

SET CLEAR GOALS

SOUND VISION

WHY DO I CARE?

HOW DO WE GET THERE?

GIVE THEM PURPOSE

CLARIFY THE GAP

FIGURE 6. FRAMEWORK FOR ORGANIZATIONAL VISION

GAME PLAN

VISION

PRE-GAME

- **Create a comprehensive list of your stakeholder types.** You can't create or achieve a Vision on your own. It can't be just your employees and customers – your success depends upon a larger ecosystem of stakeholders, so make sure you consider the broader network.

  > **Key Play:** For your list of stakeholders, define what you believe they care about most, what you think they are most afraid of, and what matters most to them.

- **Identify the most critical individual stakeholders.** While all of your stakeholders will prove to be important to your success, let's be honest, some are "more equal than others". You must understand where your power base lies, and they must have a voice in your Vision.

  > **Key Play:** Stack rank your individual stakeholders. Categorize how they influence your destiny in your role, and detail what they care about most. Moreover, identify who are the key influencers are that are the staunchest defenders of the status quo. By definition, they are the most likely obstacles that can derail your vision, and may actively create plans to neutralize it.

- **Know the bottom line.** Your Vision must support survival, not just nirvana. Be clear about the goals that must be hit for you to survive long enough to see your ship come in.

  > **Key Play:** Conduct a "pre-mortem". Imagine you have fast forwarded time to 1-5 years in the future (base the timeframe on the likely period of time that would define a fair assessment of your performance in the role you are in).

Imagine that you are being fired for poor performance. Again, using your imagination, consider all of the events that might have occurred that contributed to, and led up to, your firing. Categorize each event according to both its likelihood of occurrence, and its relative impact to your firing. Carefully consider the possible events that score high in both categories, and create plans to either mitigate their occurrence or minimize their impact.

GAME TIME

- **Engage your stakeholders.** Do not try to create your Vision on your own. People may agree with your idea, but they will believe in their own. Gather your stakeholder groups and have an external facilitator guide a discussion on what success looks like, what truly inspires them, and the goals that make the Vision real. You don't want to lead this conversation yourself – that may leave your stakeholders thinking it is your vision, not ours. Mix up stakeholder groups as much as possible when you gather them together – diverse groups will drive alignment faster.

  > **Key Play:** First, meet with your most critical stakeholders 1:1 to ensure they feel heard. Within reason, allow their concerns to set the overall agenda and the framework with which you engage your broader set of constituents.

- **Balance the Scorecard.** Challenge your stakeholders to find and create the balance. You know that business results and the larger good are symbiotic, but it is more important for them to see it. Find the balance that will create sustainability. Search for the "magic" activities that achieve both concurrently, and make those activities part of your everyday playbook.

  > **Key Play:** Once you have identified the magic activities, create a process for highlighting those examples publicly

for your organization. Give rewards and recognition to people that are unequivocally demonstrating their commitment to the Vision by their actions and accomplishments.

- **Define What it Looks Like in Action.** Have the group define the behaviors for their role in the organization that will bring the Vision to life. Your vision must be an "every day thing", not an annual thing. Every group should have a playbook for how they help fulfill the Vision. Moreover, they should understand their responsibilities to other stakeholders. When your stakeholders are truly aligned to the Vision, you have an opportunity for something great.

  > **Key Play:** Engage your Learning function, or an outside consultant, to create ways to practice executing the key behaviors that are consistent with success.

POST-GAME

- **Communicate.** As a leader, one of your most important functions is keeping the Vision front and center for the organization, and it will require more frequent communication than you think. When you have gotten to the point that you are absolutely nauseous talking about it, your stakeholders are finally starting to truly understand it.

  > **Key Play:** Create a list of your most common communication channels and key messages around your vision and design how you will share those messages across those channels over time.

- **Demonstrate.** Remember the adage, "Your actions speak so loudly that I cannot hear a word you say". From the moment you first share your vision, your stakeholders will be looking to your behavior to determine whether you really believe in it, or truly care about it. Carefully consider how your actions will be interpreted by others.

> **Key Play:** Consider your routine meetings with your team and with broader audiences. How do your actions in those venues communicate (or fail to) your vision? Also think about the previous year. What were the "moments that mattered" last year. How did you show up in those moments? Did they demonstrate a commitment to your vision? Anticipate potential high-leverage moments that are likely to occur in the next year. How would you signal your commitment to your Vision by how you show up in those moments?

• **Keep Score.** The goals you set that define your Vision will cease to matter unless you report your progress. Peter Drucker once said, "What gets measured, gets done." And to your stakeholders, what you measure, is what matters to you.

> **Key Play:** Review the metrics you report on regularly. Do they communicate your focus on your Vision? What changes would you make? Construct a dashboard that provides clarity on the metrics that define your Vision. How can you make that information more visible and readily available to all of your stakeholders?

SECTION II
STRATEGY
DESIGNING YOUR SYSTEM

STRATEGY – YOUR PATH TO ABOVE AVERAGE RETURNS

Brown Left Slot – Sprint Right Option.

This play signaled the arrival of Bill Walsh's "West Coast Offense" and the validation of his offensive strategy. While the name of this play might not be familiar to most people, many hardcore football fans know it simply as, "The Catch". "The Catch", was a touchdown pass from Joe Montana to Dwight Clark with less than a minute to go in the NFC Championship game of the 1981 season. It sealed the win for San Francisco, and sent them to their first Super Bowl, where they beat the Cincinnati Bengals, winning the first of several Lombardi trophies. Many fans argued after the game, that it was an aberration, that the play was a fluke, and that Walsh's offense was just a gimmick that would never last.

Nothing could be further from the truth. The outcome of this game shook the foundations of the power structure of the NFL, launching the 49ers into a dynastic period of nearly 20 years, and netted them 5 Super Bowl trophies. Walsh's so-called "West Coast Offense" challenged conventional football strategy, spread throughout the NFL, and still influences offensive football strategy more than 30 years later. And Brown Left Slot – Sprint Right Option was no fluke. It was the manifestation of a carefully crafted strategy.

Models for Above Average Returns

Bill Walsh's West Coast Offense offers us an interesting case example with which to explore modern business strategy. Like any strategy, its purpose is to maximize the results we can get with the resources we have. Academically put, it is a model for Above Average Returns. The phrase "above average returns" essentially acknowledges that, without an effective strategy, we will likely earn an "average return". In the game of football, that might mean that over time, we will likely lose as many games as we win, or more specifically, we will beat the teams who have inferior talent, and lose to all those whose talent is superior.

In a business context, it refers to financial returns. In its purest sense, the fundamental purpose of a business is to extract a "rent", or more plainly, a financial return, on an existing asset. That asset may be a physical asset like a plant or a building, or it could be as simple as cash. In an example of cash, the "average return" you can earn might be simply explained by the interest rate that is paid on a certificate of deposit (CD). Without any other strategy, any investor can generate that return without meaningful risk or imagination. However, to derive a higher, or "above average" return, an investor would need a strategy; perhaps created by investing in equities, bonds, real estate, etc. Alternatively, the investor would be creating a business of some sort, employing that asset in some type of business model that generates a return. The strategy he or she employed, and how effectively it is executed, will determine whether the return is above average, or not.

From an academic perspective, strategy is often represented by unique approaches to achieving above average returns. Two common models are the Resource Model and the Industrial Organizational Model, which focus on issues either internal or external to the organization, respectively. While it may be a significant oversimplification of the comprehensive study behind these models, they simply represent how you choose to focus, and around what you choose to build your strategy; the unique resources you have available to you, or the external markets you choose to play in. In the next few chapters we will explore both of these models in detail, and look for inspiration from some of the great football strategists for inspiration on how you can achieve above average returns in your business.

STRATEGY - MITIGATING YOUR WEAKNESSES

The Resource Model for Above Average Returns

With the Resource Model for Above Average Returns, essentially, you are looking internally, focusing on the unique resources or capabilities of the assets you have at your disposal. It is based on these key assumptions:

- Each firm is defined by its unique collection resources and capabilities, which provide the basis of its strategy, and ultimately determine the return they will generate

- Firms collect different resources and assets over time, and thus develop their own unique approach or strategy to create competitive advantage

- Resources may not be highly mobile across firms

The Resource model is very straightforward and practical. It rests on the concept that your strategy is largely determined by the assets that you have. In football, you would probably not choose a power running offense if you happened to have the best quarterback and receivers in the league. In business, if your asset was a wheelbarrow, you would more likely start a dirt hauling business rather than a house painting business to achieve a return on your wheelbarrow asset.

Over time, firms tend to differentiate themselves over time by the people and assets they assemble over time. Football teams acquire talent through annual college recruiting or through the NFL draft to develop the roster of people that they will need to bring their vision to fruition. From a business perspective, as they grow, organizations may build and develop intellectual property like technology assets.

The issue of mobility of assets is an important aspect of the Resource Model. In college football, mobility of talent is very restrictive. Teams can collect and hoard the best talent, and there are restrictive rules that limit the ability of players to change schools. In the world of business, restricting mobility of assets is much more difficult, given anti-monopoly laws and the effects of globalization. But, certain provisions, like patent law, allow for firms to create unique assets and restrict their mobility, and thus, to create unique resource-based strategies to extract above average returns.

I discuss this model first, simply because it is the approach most people, and most large enterprises for that matter, are most comfortable and familiar with. It involves taking a careful inventory of the firm, and assessing its strengths and weaknesses.

And while intuitively, we might imagine that focusing on the inherent strengths of the organization as a foundation of strategy makes the most sense – and of course it does – I would posit that most game-changing strategies, and therefore perhaps the most instructive ones, come from a careful and honest examination of the firm's weaknesses.

 Coaching Point: While your Resources tend to define the strategies chosen for organizations, true game-changing strategies are inspired by your weaknesses.

Revisiting "The Catch"

In 1981, The Dallas Cowboys were the class of the NFC. Over the past decade or so, the Cowboys had become "America's Team", winning championships while demonstrating a palpable level of swagger. They were based in a high-profile city, with its own self-named hit TV show, and played in a stadium with a whole cut in the roof – ostensibly "so God could watch them play". They were owned by a wealthy oil man, who ensured that they had the best of everything. Even their cheerleaders were a national phenomenon.

But the Dallas Cowboys were more than just sizzle. They were coached by Tom Landry, who revolutionized many aspects of the modern game, and ultimately landed in the Hall of Fame. He was joined in the Hall by 7 of his players that played in the 70's, validating their place as one of the great teams in NFL history.

Certainly, their defense had a lot to do with that standard excellence. While Dallas employed a somewhat unique approach to defensive line play, referred to as the Flex, they played a traditional style of defense for the era. It was based on a 4-3 scheme (four defensive lineman with three linebackers behind them) which focused on stopping the run first, then attacking passers with aggressive blitzing. This defensive philosophy was a trademark of American football in the 60's and 70's, and was designed to force the opponent to pass the football, increasing the opportunity for turnovers. And, if you had the elite level of defensive players the Cowboys had, this style of defense would render a traditional, conservative offense, basically inert.

Unfortunately for Dallas, that defensive philosophy was a recipe for disaster when facing Walsh's offense. With a pass-first approach, Dallas' Flex - characterized by a slight delay for a "read and react" by the defensive line designed to close down running lanes - simply provided Joe Montana with another half second to get his feet set and read the defense. The short routes and quick passes rendered the vaunted Dallas pass rush ineffective. And finally, the designed waggles — quarterback rollouts — neutralized the effectiveness of Dallas' greatest defensive weapon, defensive end, Ed "Too Tall" Jones. By rolling out, Montana would have clearer sight lines, opening up new passing lanes, instead of trying to pass directly over the 6'8" Jones.

All of those elements came together in the 1982 NFC Championship. While the game ended in a narrow win for the 49ers with a last second touchdown, the 49ers dominated the game offensively. They outgained the Cowboys by over 150 yards, dominated the time of possession, and Montana was the game's Most Valuable Player, completing 3 touchdown passes.

Walsh's plan culminated with Brown Left Slot – Sprint Right Option, the late touchdown pass to Dwight Clark. Clark was a prototypical wide receiver in Walsh's offense – a disciplined route runner with excellent hands. While many Cowboy fans might like to believe that the catch Jones made over Everett Walls was a fluke, those familiar with Walsh's offense know better. The play is designed to create multiple options for Montana, who would be in a designed "Sprint Right". He would have the choice of Roger Craig in the short right flat, Freddy Solomon on a hook on the right side, and if neither of those two were open, Jones could be found running horizontally behind the action. Montana knew exactly where to throw the ball, and the play unfolded exactly as it was drawn up.

The Catch was the ratification of Walsh's offensive system, and the demise of old school defenses as we knew them. But at the time, most casual fans did not recognize that there had been a changing of the guard. But Walsh did. However, the lesson for us lies in how that strategy was formulated.

The birth of a new offensive strategy

In 1979, Bill Walsh was hired to take over as Head Coach and General Manager for the San Francisco 49ers, after they had posted the worst record in the NFL the year before. He inherited a depleted roster, and the entire franchise was in a shambles. The 49ers repeated the 2-14 won-loss record in Walsh's first year, and despite meaningful improvement, another losing season in 1980 left even Walsh wondering whether his strategy would work. But he had seen this strategy work before. Because despite it later being called the "West Coast Offense", he had actually invented it during his tenure in Cincinnati over a decade before.

At that time, he was the offensive coordinator for the Bengals, working for head coach Paul Brown. Brown was a legend in his own right already, with one NFL franchise named after him in Cleveland, and well on his way to building another one in Cincinnati. He is credited with many innovations that are now part of the modern game, but his offensive and defensive philosophies were rooted in the fundamentals. His teams focused on trying to run the ball, and to stop the opponent from doing the same, and his formations were indicative of the game in the 50s and 60s, because, well, many coaches at the time patterned their philosophies after Brown.

As such, Brown was a traditionalist. He favored a 2-back power offense, and vertical passing game designed to stretch the defense, forcing defensive backs to maintain a safe distance away from the line of scrimmage to open up running lanes for his backs. And this was the system that he installed when he launched the Bengals in 1968. He hired Walsh due to his broad base of experience, his exposure to many strong football coaches, but mainly because of his demonstrated deep understanding of Sid Gillman's vertical passing game.

But that passing game required a prototypical QB with a strong arm, which could deliver passes downfield with enough velocity to force the defensive backs to respect those deep routes. Without that type of skill at quarterback, defensive backs were free to move forward to stifle shorter routes and help out in run defense. Without that type of threat at quarterback, Paul Brown's offense just wouldn't be effective.

So, in the 1969 draft, the Bengals selected Greg Cook, a local Ohio football hero, who grew up in Chillicothe, and played college football at the University of Cincinnati. Cook was a rare talent, with all of the requisite tools. He took over as the starting quarterback in his first NFL game – quite unusual for that era, but Cook had a unique combination of physical gifts and an advanced understanding of the game for a rookie. He led the Bengals to a startling 3-0 start, in only their second season as an expansion team. But in that third game, Cook tore his rotator cuff (before that was a known diagnosis), and sat out the next three games. He returned, and despite missing those games, led the NFL in passing his rookie season, with a torn rotator cuff. This fact both boggles the mind, and speaks to Cook's immense physical talent.

Despite his short tenure, Walsh would later comment that Greg Cook was the most talented quarterback he ever saw. Had he not suffered that injury, Walsh may have never been forced to innovate and create his new offense. But Walsh was not that fortunate. Cook had surgery in the offseason, was placed on injured reserve, and never really returned.

As such, going into the 1970 season, Walsh was faced with trying to run his offense without a competent quarterback to guide it. After being unsatisfied with what he saw in training camp, he picked up Virgil Carter in a trade with the Chicago Bears, where he had spent two relatively unremarkable seasons. After bringing him in and working with him, Walsh recognized that Carter didn't have the arm strength to stretch the defenses and execute their vertical passing offense effectively. Moreover, as a recent expansion team, he didn't have the quality or depth on his offensive line to dominate the line of scrimmage to enable a successful running game.

Confronted with those facts, he recognized that he was ill-prepared to execute the system favored by Brown, and taught to him by Al Davis and Sid Gillman. His concerns were well-founded, as the Bengals went 1-6 in their first 7 games. Walsh was going to need a new strategy.

 Coaching Point: Don't wait until periodic meetings to revisit strategy. Sieze the energy provided by major changes to create new opportunities.

SWOT Analysis

While Walsh was always considered a cerebral coach, I doubt that he pulled out a strategy textbook to research the Resource Model for Above Average Returns while crafting what would become the most innovative new offensive strategy of the modern era. But I will wager that he utilized a very effective strategy process called a SWOT analysis. It is probably the most commonly-known strategy formulation tool, and also one of the simplest. A SWOT Analysis is simply a careful inventory of your Strengths, Weaknesses, Opportunities and Threats (SWOT). But that does not undermine its power to provide insights, and we will explore it a bit more deeply in this chapter.

Fundamentally, you are identifying issues that are either helpful or harmful to your success, from both an internal and external perspective. It is most commonly represented in a 2x2 matrix as shown below:

	Helpful	Harmful
Internal	**Strengths**	**Weaknesses**
External	**Opportunities**	**Threats**

FIGURE 7. SWOT FRAMEWORK

So, his known Weaknesses in personnel forced Walsh to take a careful of the internal resources he had available to him. As such, he was focused primarily on the top half of the matrix above; honestly assessing his current Weaknesses, but also looking for potential Strengths that he could exploit in his revamped strategy. His analysis might have looked something like this:

Strengths	Weaknesses
Strong organizational foundation with Paul Brown as head coach	Lack of quality and depth on the offensive line
Accurate thrower in Carter	Inability to stretch the field with downfield passing
Capable young running back with ability to catch as well as run	Shorter QB that will have difficulty seeing over the line
Disciplined route runner in TE Bob Trumpy	No speed at Wide Receiver
Mobile quarterback that throws well on the run	Inability to hold back a pass rush for a standard 7 step drop

FIGURE 8. STRENGTHS AND WEAKNESSES OF THE 1970 CINCINNATI BENGALS

The "Ohio River Offense"

So, with this analysis in hand, formulated during that stretch of losses to begin the 1970 season, Walsh began tinkering with a radically different strategy for the Bengals; an approach that would take advantages of the strengths he had, and mitigate the weaknesses.

Key elements of his new system;

- Shortening the drop back of the quarterback from a traditional 7 steps, to a 5-step, and often a 3-step drop, to minimize the impact of his offensive line's shortcomings

- Widening the splits of his wide receivers to move defensive backs further away from the tackle box to weaken their ability to help in run support

- Those wider splits also created wider horizontal pass route lanes, forcing defensive backs to cover more area

- Horizontal passing routes that would force linebackers into pass coverage, and inhibit their ability to fill gaps in the defensive line

- Putting the quarterback in motion; sprinting him outside of the tackle box, enabling new sight lanes, and forcing linebackers into accounting for the quarterback instead of just pass coverage

- Shorter, easier passes with a much higher completion rate that would turn the passing game into a conservative option, that was fulfilled by running plays in traditional offenses

- Getting running backs and wide receivers the ball in open space, often running horizontally against defenses that are often defined by their vertical responsibilities, and forcing defenses to make tackles in open space

 Coaching Point: Innovative strategy development often begins by focusing more on what you can do, than only on what you cannot do.

This approach transformed the passing game into a conservative, ball-control methodology, as opposed to a high-risk/high-reward tool. Once fully-installed, the Bengals never lost again the rest of the regular season, reeling off seven straight victories and earning a spot in the playoffs – the first expansion team in NFL history to do so within their first three seasons. Under Walsh's direction in Cincinnati, three different quarterbacks would lead the NFL in various statistical categories. While it became known as the "West Coast Offense" a decade or so later, Walsh's system was born on the banks of the Ohio River in Cincinnati. And, it was born from a careful inventory of his organization's strengths and weaknesses.

Innovating to mitigate weaknesses

By honestly assessing the weaknesses of his organization, Walsh was able to use those constraints as the fuel for the innovation needed to develop a new strategy. This is a tried and true method for successful innovation;

- Be clear about your ultimate goal, but let go of preconceived notions of how you must get there

- Question every other accepted "truth"

- List out the known constraints, and focus on changing everything else

- To test the validity of a new idea, simply ask yourself "what must be true?", instead of wondering "why it won't work"

Walsh's goals were simple. As an offensive coordinator, he had three requirements;

- *Score points.* You only win the game by scoring more than the other team.

- *Protect the football.* Statistically, since scoring without offensive possession of the football is infrequent and unusual, it is very difficult to win football games if you turn the ball over – throwing interceptions or fumbling.

- *Control the clock.* Maintaining possession by executing prolonged drives. This increases the likelihood of scoring, and keeps your defense fresh, while exhausting theirs. Again, a high statistical correlation to winning games.

So to be successful in creating a new strategy, Walsh had to keep those "non-negotiables" in mind, but allow himself to consider all other alternatives. The first step is to question accepted truths. Consider some of the truisms that his approach upended;

- *Passing plays were high risk, and were to be used only when necessary, or to keep defenses honest in their zone responsibilities.* By creating more space through formation, and throwing shorter passes, Walsh created a high-percentage pass offense that could achieve the same end goal, prolonged drives, of a rush-heavy attack.

- *You use success in the running game to set up success in the passing game.* Walsh turned this upside-down, using passing plays as his core, and running plays as his change of pace. With defenses spreading out to block passing lanes, he opened up running lanes that would otherwise be filled.

- *Passing routes were timed to be 3-5 seconds in length.* The Gillman-Coryell system that even Walsh was raised on, was predicated on the idea that you had to provide the quarterback a minimum of 3-5 seconds to get through a 5 to 7 step drop to get set and throw the football. Walsh's designed 3 step drops were able to deliver the football 1-2 seconds faster.

- *You don't throw a 3 yard pass, when you need 6 yards for a first down.* Walsh proved that receivers running horizontally and catching passes at full speed could reliably generate significant yards after the catch (YAC – an acronym that did not exist before Walsh), and force defenses into pass coverage nightmares.

Walsh was successful in developing this new strategy by refusing to accept limitations as dead ends. While accepting that he could not throw long, he realized he could throw short. His running backs couldn't get rushing yards, but they could get receiving yards. He couldn't get behind the defense with his passing game, but he could throw it in front of them, and make them chase it.

Then, to test the validity of his ideas, he then had to identify what must be true for this approach to work. This system was a radical departure for traditional offenses, and reduced the need for a tall, strong-armed quarterback who could sit in the pocket and execute a vertical passing game. But, for it to work, it would demand a new set of skills and capabilities. For his new offense to be successful, certain conditions would have to exist;

- *The quarterback would have to be accurate.* To maintain ball control with a passing attack, you simply cannot miss all that often.

- *The quarterback would have to be mobile.* The offense's designed roll-outs and waggles would require a quarterback to complete passes while moving.

- *The quarterback would have to be patient and smart.* The system was built upon multiple route options that would open up in a planned time progression. The quarterback will need to proceed through a defined decision tree.

- *You would need solid route runners.* The new philosophy minimized the need for downfield speed, but necessitated precise routes to ensure they were at the right place, at the right time.

- *The system would favor bigger receivers and tight ends.* The horizontal routes were often going to create opportunities for missed tackles and long gains, but there would also be big collisions that smaller receivers may not be able to sustain.

 Coaching Point: When you are developing innovative strategy, don't focus on what "why it won't work". Instead, ask yourself, or better yet, your team, "What would have to be true for this to work?"

Going back to Walsh's initial analysis of his Strengths and Weaknesses, he realized that he had the tools to execute his plan. He had a mobile, accurate, experienced quarterback, and a talented route runner at tight end. Moreover, he was confident that the strong coaching staff under Paul Brown could assist him in coaching this new approach; as the system minimizes the need for overwhelming physical skills but puts significant pressure on the coaching staff to coach the required execution and precision.

Obviously, any football fan knows how successful this system has been. It was the foundation for multiple Super Bowl wins for the San Francisco 49ers, as well as for several coaches who apprenticed under Walsh, and ultimately, it revolutionized offensive football. And like many innovations, the insights that he uncovered proved to be more than just a band-aid to temporarily shore up his weaknesses. They ultimately proved to the foundation of an entirely new offensive philosophy.

Creating new companies by identifying your lack of Resources

This is a powerful mindset that has spawned many innovative strategies that have allowed organizations to overcome weaknesses, both to create new companies and to evolve existing ones. One well-known case example is Dell Computers. Dell was started in Austin,

Texas back in the early 80s, by Michael Dell[17]. At that time, IBM and its competitors were selling personal computers in retail electronics stores like Radio Shack. The PC was new, and the general assumption was that customers would need to talk to someone in person to help them with the sale, and that they would need to see, touch and feel the product to understand it well enough to buy it. As such, you would need to have enough inventory to fill stores with product, and that would require significant capital. Moreover, as a new product, the accepted thought was that customers would only trust well-known brands enough to trigger a sale, given how expensive they were at the time.

But Dell had spent time in his high school years taking apart computers to truly understand how they worked. In his early college years, he became familiar enough with computer components to start a business selling computer parts and upgrade kits. As such, he soon became aware of the true cost of materials for a personal computer, and realized that the large companies that were building PCs – driven by their high overheads and the complex supply chains they employed - were driving up the cost. So, he knew there was margin to be made by simplifying the process and going direct to the consumer.

And that margin was the driving force. His goal as a pure entrepreneur is to create an above average return on investment. Personal computing was his chosen market due to its attractive margins. But he was short on resources. He didn't have a manufacturing line, nor did he have the money to create one. And even if he did, he didn't have the capital to create the inventory necessary to break into the channel dominated by Apple, IBM, Commodore, and the like. So he began to question every accepted "truth" about the industry of building and marketing personal computers.

. . . .

[17](Various, Michael Dell, n.d.)

- *Personal computers must be sold in stores.*

  > What if people bought them direct from the manufacturer, placing orders over the phone like many other types of products?

- *You must be able to train the retail channel to sell your products with an army of field sales and marketing people, before I make even one sale.*

  > If I sell direct, I can train my people myself, ensuring they are experts on my products alone, and can scale up as I grow.

- *You need to create a broad assortment of SKUs to offer all of the variations that a customer may need.*

  > If I sell direct, I can configure the system according to customer needs.

- *You must have ready boxed inventory so a customer can buy it and take it home immediately.*

  > As a new category, PCs were not an intrinsic part of everyday business and home life yet. In exchange for a lower price, and the ability to customize, customers would be willing to wait for a week or so to get their product.

- *I must have a significant capital position to secure enough components to build the necessary inventory.*

  > If I sell direct, I can use the customer's money to finance my growth, as I will collect the sales revenue before building the product.

After challenging these truths, he examined what must be true for the new approach to be successful;

- *Focused marketing.* He would not have the brand awareness to pursue the broad market at first, so he would have to pursue niche segments;

> *Margin sensitive industries.* One of his first segments he pursued was the government, where low price for clear specifications would win the day.

> *Hobbyists or computer-savvy people.* These groups would embrace the opportunity to embrace the opportunity to design its components and specifications.

- *Talented, aggressive sales force.* Without a big marketing budget, he would need people who can sell over the phone, and close business.

- *Significant human capital requirements.* This strategy would require a dedicated, technically-competent staff to work with customers, assemble systems, and provide support. He would be asking a lot from his people.

As anyone who was around for the technology boom of the 1990s knows, the strategy worked extremely well. Dell established a beachhead winning government contracts, and the Government segment is still one of Dell's most profitable units. Dell became known for their sales organization – taking hungry young people, investing in their training, and developing them into highly-competent salespeople. Dell's early employees were fiercely loyal, "do whatever it takes" people that often worked for stock when the company had difficulty meeting payroll. They fostered a strong execution culture that persists today. Those early employees retired early, on the back of those early stock options making them all millionaires, or "Dellionaires", as they have been referred to in Austin. Moreover, since the technology was evolving so quickly, many of Dell's competitors and retail partners were feeling the pain of significant markdowns as stronger, faster units were appearing on the market every 6 months. Dell's minimal inventory model shielded them from this cost. Finally, and perhaps most importantly, the negative cash conversion cycle model (the cash conversion cycle measures the length of time it takes to convert a sale into cash. Dell's was negative, as they received pre-payment from customers and received payment terms from suppliers) that Dell's model enabled, created exponential wealth in the high growth period for personal computers. While its competitors were burning more and more cash to create the inventory to reach the retail segments, Dell was using capital from its customers, inverting its cost of capital, and allowing it to deliver attractive net margins despite offering lower prices. These factors combined to create significantly above average stock investment returns, and created meaningful wealth for shareholders. And it started because Michael Dell focused on what his weaknesses were, and innovated around them with a new strategy.

 Coaching Point: Financial returns can come from many different business models. Don't force fit your strategy into just one option.

While not specifically financial in nature, Walsh had similar success. Before it was nicknamed the "West Coast Offense", he found significant success in Cincinnati. His quarterbacks would lead the NFL in several passing categories, his offenses set records, and an expansion team reached the playoffs in only its third year of existence. Only the presence of the Steelers in their division, in the midst of one of the great dynasties in sports, blocked Walsh's Bengal teams from more storied success.

But he would find that success in San Francisco. In 1979 he would take over the 49ers, and he immediately installed his system. But as the Resource Model of Above Average Returns states, your resources dictate strategy. And in this case, the quarterback he inherited, Steve DeBerg, was simply not accurate enough to direct this offense. Given the friction of mobility of resources defined by the NFL, Walsh had to wait to get the key resource he needed to drive his strategy, and build them over time. But, the next year, he drafted a skinny quarterback with suspect arm strength (rated 6 out of 10 at the NFL combine) in the third round, named Joe Montana. But he was smart, extremely accurate, deceptively mobile, and threw well on the run. In that same draft, they waited until the 10th round to select Dwight Clark, who despite his lack of vertical speed, was 6'4" tall, carried a larger frame, ran precise routes, and had great hands. He knew what he needed to run his system. And he knew that Clark would be open in the back of the end zone, and that he would make "The Catch".

CHALK TALK

Identifying your Weaknesses

- Identify your weaknesses by comprehensively examining your organization from multiple angles.

    > Financial resources. This includes revenue streams, investments, diversified income, and grants.

    > Physical items. Consider buildings and equipment that you rent or own.

    > Intellectual property. Patents, copyrights, and trademarks fall into this area.

    > Human resources. Think of your employees, volunteers, and mentors.

    > Key players. Think of vital personnel to your business.

    > Employee programs. Think of any programs that help your employees excel.

    > Company workflow. This includes best work practices.

    > Company culture. This is the environment that your employees work in.

    > Company reputation. Think of how your business has grown its reputation.

    > Market position. You'll consider how your business fits in the overall market.

> > Growth potential. Think of how your business is positioned for future growth.

- Be honest and transparent. Sugar coating issues or spinning them will kill your ability to react effectively.

Innovating around them

- Be clear about your goals, but be flexible about how you achieve them

- List out the known constraints, and focus on changing everything else

- Question every other accepted "truth"

- For it to be different that you think, ask yourself "what must be true?"

STRATEGY - MAXIMIZING STRENGTHS

Only the Paranoid Survive

Not every great strategy is borne out of desperation, but there are often some significant impediments in your way. Simply put, when you have a strong set of resources, there is very little impetus to self-examine. Common sense would say that when you have a strong position, your job is not to innovate, but simply to execute. But the landscape is littered with companies that rode out a string of successes until it was too late. Andy Grove, the former CEO of Intel once said, "Success breeds complacency. Complacency breeds failure. Only the paranoid survive." He drove the company to continuously test new ideas and strategies, and challenged his entire leadership to do the same. But how do you rationalize altering your strategy when you have been successful?

Maximizing existing resources

In 2002, the Texas Longhorns had just completed another successful season, their second consecutive with 11 wins, and a top 10 ranking. Coach Mack Brown's recruiting prowess was becoming legendary, and the roster seemed stacked for years to come. They had a perennially strong passing offense, recently led by NFL-bound Chris

Simms, and now had Chance Mock, a former Parade All-American quarterback, ready to go. Texas' offensive coordinator, Greg Davis, was committed to a pro-style offense that flourished under Simms and seemed well-suited to Mock, who had the requisite accuracy and decision-making that was required for success. The team returned the most talented receiver set in the country, so Mock appeared to be ready to pick up right where Simms left off. They had the talent they needed to execute their offensive strategy, and were primed for success.

However, the Longhorns also had a young redshirt freshman quarterback, Vince Young, who represented a unique talent. College football had not seen a quarterback that big and that fast, and those attributes made him a devastating runner. However, Young was raw and unpolished as a passer, and would often struggle with the fundamentals that were required in Davis' offense. His raw talent was undeniable, but those talents were not being exploited in the pro-style offense that they had fully committed to over the last six years. After some time, Mack Brown insisted that he get on the field sharing time with Mock.

 Coaching Point: Be watchful for resources that are being underutilized by your current strategy.

Taking risks even though you are at the top

Meanwhile, at West Virginia University, head coach Rich Rodriguez, had dual-threat running quarterback, and was finding success with an offense he called the Zone Read. It was an interesting twist to an option-style running attack that was designed to take advantage of a quarterback who could run. Like most option offenses, it is designed to isolate one defender, purposefully leaving him unblocked. The scheme directs an offensive player with the ball to run toward that player, and essentially exercise an "option" – choosing from multiple choices of running, pitching, or passing based on the behavior of that player. In the Zone Read, the quarterback has the option, and after taking the snap, he begins the play prepared to hand the ball to a running back running to his left or right. The quarterback extends the ball for the runner to take, while he "reads" the defensive end, determining whether that defender appears to be attacking the runner or himself. When the quarterback determines which, he either hands the ball to the back, or keeps it and runs it himself, to avoid the defender. Additionally, he can choose to do neither, and step back and pass the ball. A physically gifted quarterback can create nightmares for defenses with this attack.

However, the Zone Read represented a significant shift away from a pro-style offense, which would require wholesale changes for every position on the field, and an entirely new nomenclature and a play structure. And given its run focus, it had different approaches to down and distance, and an entirely new set of "reads' for his quarterback. These are the kind of changes that are almost solely introduced after a coaching change. But at the very least, this type of change would be installed in the offseason, never in the middle of a season.

 Coaching Point: Remember the quote from Picasso, "Good artists copy. Great artists steal." Be attentive to other successful strategies and see what you can steal from them.

But after studying the offense more closely, the possibilities presented by Vince Young in this type of system were just too intriguing. After consulting with Rodriguez and other coaches familiar with this option offense, he installed it at Texas midseason of the 2004 season. The stakes were high. These are the kinds of moves that if unsuccessful, make you look desperate and foolish, and often get you fired. But if your goal is a championship – not just to be good – as a coach, your job is to find ways to maximize your strengths to give yourself the best chance to win them all.

After one bumpy game against Missouri, where Young was essentially learning on the job, Young exploded against Texas Tech. He passed and ran for 300 total yards, scoring 5 touchdowns, and the offense put 51pts on the board. Texas won the rest of their games that season, including an epic postseason matchup against Michigan in the Rose Bowl, where Young set new records for that historic venue. Moreover, Young never lost another game in college, ripping off 20 straight wins, including the National Championship Game after the 2005 season.

 Coaching Point: Be willing to experiment with new strategies even during, perhaps especially during, periods of success.

The Longhorns were already a top 10 program, but it was their willingness to experiment at the height of that success that ultimately allowed them to win a national championship. Radical shifts like this while at the top of an industry, represents significant risk for the leader of that organization. Anyone who is familiar with college football, especially at a program like The University of Texas, understands the level of scrutiny that Mack Brown was opening himself up to. But great leaders and organizations are constantly exploring, evaluating, and experimenting to ensure they stay at the top.

The VRIO framework

Clearly, Vince Young represented a unique resource that warranted making the radical change in offensive philosophy. But how do you know if your "resource" is such a Strength – such that it warrants a change in strategy, and worth taking a risk to fully exploit it? The VRIO framework[18] may be a useful tool to help you test it.

The VRIO model can help you determine whether your resource can really be a source of competitive advantage. It asks you to assess whether that resource is; Valuable, Rare, Hard to Imitate, and a fit for your Organization.

. . . .

[18](Barney & Hesterly, 2011)

Valuable	Rare	Imitable	Organizational Fit
Does a resource enable a firm to exploit an environmental opportunity, and/ or neutralize an environmental threat?	Is a resource currently controlled by only a small number of competing firms?	Do firms without a resource face a cost disadvantage in obtaining or developing it?	Are a firm's other policies and procedures organized to support the exploitation of its valuable, rare, and costly-to-imitate resources?

FIGURE 9. THE VRIO FRAMEWORK

Applying it to the Texas Longhorns case above, Vince Young clearly passes the VRIO test;

- *Valuable* – Vince Young's skill set combined the three prized capabilities in offensive football; the speed to run past someone, the agility to elude tacklers, and the size and strength to run over them. These skills are highly valued regardless of offensive philosophy.

- *Rare* – Possessing one of those attributes at Young's level is enough to secure a starting position on a team. Combining all three, and doing so as a quarterback is indeed rare.

- *Ability to Imitate.* Teams learn to defend offensive systems by having their backups perform like the opponent, providing defenses an opportunity to practice what they will see and do in the upcoming game. No opponent had anyone who could imitate Vince Young, and as such, defenses were never fully prepared for what they would see on the field.

- *Organizational Fit.* While the shift in offensive philosophy was meaningful, the Longhorns had a premier-level offensive line, and Cedric Benson at running back to complement Young in the option-style offense. So, while it represented change, the Longhorns had the right type of skills around Young to make it work.

Regardless of how compelling Young's talent was, it is important to note how different the situation Mack Brown and Bill Walsh faced. Walsh was operating from a position of weakness. The stakes were low, and he was forced to do something drastic. Brown had every reason to play it safe. Each situation is different, and the right strategy will be dependent on your unique circumstances, but it is critical to be honest with the actual strengths or weaknesses of your assets.

Truly valuable?

In the world of business, the strategies of technology companies have historically been built around the Resource Model, deriving a competitive advantage on the strength of their innovative technology. Google has leveraged their core capability around search into a wide range of opportunities and business models. Cisco's technology around managing data across a network has delivered outstanding shareholder value for decades. Both companies have created valuable assets that have been the driver of above average returns.

But just as frequently, technology companies have misjudged the value of their resources. A couple of decades before the DVD emerged as the standard in video storage and playback, Pioneer, in partnership with Philips and MCA, launched the LaserDisc. It was far superior in quality compared to VHS, and they felt that it would replace the VHS format that had only been on the market for a couple of years. But both the players and the media were meaningfully more expensive than VHS. Pioneer was certain that their technology was superior, and thus more valuable, and they would win in the marketplace.

But they forgot the one key axiom about value. Something is worth only what someone is willing to pay for it. While that sounds simplistic, it is a key concept that many organizations forget when they are assessing their own assets, and evaluating their strengths. The only meaningful measure of value is determined by the customer. In this case, the cost differential was too high to rationalize someone adopting the LaserDisc as their player of choice. The quality difference was not big enough, or quite simply, not valued enough by the consumer to pay the premium. To the home video customer in the late 70s, the LaserDisc was not Valuable.

Put quite simply, something is only as valuable as whatever someone is willing to pay for it at a given time. While that seems trivial or a bit esoteric, it still is the source of a lot of bad strategy and pricing decisions. Take the example of selling your house. When you decide to sell, inevitably, you think about how much you paid for it, and how much you have invested in it since then. You think about all of the improvements you have made, and all of the value you have added to the property and dwelling. But when you contact a real estate agent, they listen politely and then tell you that your house is worth exactly what other houses like yours in the neighborhood are selling for – no more, no less. You argue that your house has so many unique features that are going to drive up the price. But you are looking at it from your perspective – the cost basis you uniquely understand, and how you value the improvements. Ultimately, you may be right, but only the ultimate buyer's assessment matters.

There is an established axiom in behavioral economics referred to as the "endowment effect". It describes the circumstance that people ascribe more value to things than others might, simply because they own them. So, as you assess your resources to determine your Strengths, you must consider strengths only from the perspective of the customer. Are they paying a premium for them in the marketplace now? If it is a new business model, what corollary can you draw on that would make you believe that customers will pay a premium for access to your valuable asset in the future? Your ability to evaluate this accurately will largely determine your success in allocating resources, and winning in the marketplace.

Bringing it back to football, value is determined by your production on the field and measured by the numbers on the scoreboard. You are only as good as your last game, and ultimately, just like in business, you will be judged on your production. Vince Young was only a VRIO asset with the appropriate strategy applied. The purpose of strategy is to translate potential into production, but confusing potential for true value for too long can be damaging.

 Coaching Point: Assets are only as valuable as customers' willingness to pay for them, or the results you can create with them – no more, no less.

Intel represents a meaningful case to explain the how a company can exploit its resources to deliver an above average return. Intel began as a company specializing in memory chips, but upon the emergence of the IBM personal computer, focused primarily on microprocessors. As the PC category exploded, several companies challenged their position in the market, but Intel's expertise and focus helped them maintain leadership. After several iterations, they landed on the Pentium processor core which became the de facto standard for the PC industry, and helped them be part of the "Wintel (Microsoft Windows + Intel chips)" platform that has dominated the personal computer marketplace for over thirty years – an eon in the technology space.

Clearly, the Pentium chip represents a VRIO asset;

- *Valuable* – It represented the single most expensive part in the PC platform that was selling millions of units per year, and growing geometrically for a couple of decades.

- *Rare* – The combination of the processing capabilities of the Pentium chip, combined with its extensibility and system integration made it unique in the world of computing.

- *Ability to Imitate.* The development of a new semiconductor chip core, like the Pentium, costs billions to create, refine, and drive adoption. So, that barrier to entry made it very hard to imitate.

- *Organizational Fit.* The Pentium platform represented a perfect manifestation of Intel's core capabilities, culture and purpose. It was a combination of technical innovation and manufacturing excellence and efficiency.

The power of that VRIO asset vaulted the market capitalization of Intel to over $300B at one point, and has helped it maintain a value of over $100B during that entire period – a level of consistency unusual for the technology industry.

Truly Inimitable?

But as history as shown us, rare assets that are impossible to imitate, are truly rare indeed. Since the dawn of the technology age, the ability to maintain a competitive advantage with technology, or any other product or service feature for that matter, is nearly impossible. If the margins are attractive enough, competitors will find a way to match your product or service, and aided by globalization, are doing so more quickly year after year. While most will innovate to create something unique, we have seen companies all over the world seemingly steal intellectual property to create near carbon copies of leading products and services, and do so with impunity. Patent holders may pound on the desk, but most companies cannot successfully defend these competitive forces, and if their only strength is that resource they feel is Inimitable, then they will often lose. This is a dynamic that is accelerating in today's global economy, and there is no reason to think the paradigm will ever reverse.

So what was the secret of Intel's staying power, and the source of the Strength that generated above average returns for so long? You can find it buried in Moore's Law[19], an axiom accredited to Gordon Moore, co-founder of Intel. Simply put, it essentially predicted that semiconductor performance would double every 18 months for the

. . . .

[19](Various, Moore's Law, n.d.)

foreseeable future; that essentially his product would improve exponentially, on a relatively consistent basis, for years to come.

Now it is important to note that Moore's Law is not based on a physical or natural law. It is simply an observation and a projection from a person and a company that is ultimately responsible for delivering on it, through the power of their own execution. In many ways you could consider such a commitment to be unrealistic at worst, and at best, ill-advised. Even if you could meet such lofty expectations, why would you want to? As a market leader, wouldn't you want to slow it down and extract those returns over a longer period of time? Wouldn't that be the best strategy to deliver sustainable, above average returns? Well, it certainly speaks to Andy Grove's quote about paranoia, and its reflection on the Intel company culture. They accepted that technological advantages are fleeting, and that most rare resources are sooner or later, imitated. So, in this case of the Pentium platform, the truly rare and Inimitable resource was Intel's commitment to continuous improvement, and their unique competencies around product development and manufacturing. Their capability and commitment to continuously improve was what made their Resource Model-based strategy work.

The converse is also true, and there are too many examples to list here. But, consider these case examples;

- Motorola was too slow in creating a replacement for its wildly successful Razr phone, and within a startlingly short period of time, was completely out of the mobile phone industry – a technology the company pioneered

- Similarly, RIM Technologies innovated on the mobile phone platform, adding a full keyboard in its line of Blackberry products. Despite being a de facto standard for enterprise environments, they rode the success of that platform too long, and by refusing to embrace the opportunity of touch screen technology, are now almost a business anachronism

So the takeaway for us here is to challenge ourselves around how unique our resources really are, and to accept the likelihood that most of our competitive advantages we currently hold, will disappear over time. Our ability and commitment to continuously evolving our resources – reevaluating, benchmarking, continuously improving, and innovating them, will be the true strength that will generate above average returns.

Like the technology industry, and business in general, football is a game based on fleeting competitive advantage. When one team is successful at doing something, opposing coaches will get into the film room and painstakingly break down what you are doing. As Pablo Picasso is famous for saying, "Good artists copy, great artists steal". Very quickly, they will copy what you are doing, and/or develop a new offensive or defensive strategy to neutralize it. In the world of football, there are no patents – no way to protect a great idea. So much so, that coaches routinely teach other coaches what they are doing over the offseason. It is demonstrable proof that they know that there is no secret play or scheme that will provide a reliable competitive advantage. Their success will be predicated on their ability to;

- Understand that the ultimate arbiter of the strength of your asset will be determined on the field, or in the case of a business, by your customers

- Continuously review their unique assets to determine if there is another, better way to extract value for the organization; regardless of, and perhaps especially when, how successful they currently are

- Recognize that the only resource that can provide a sustained competitive advantage is the willingness to continuously evolve and improve that resource to ensure they stay one step ahead of the competition

- Choose strategies that are consistent with their vision, purpose, and organization capabilities

And ultimately, reaching the pinnacle in both football and business is what is truly rare. And, it all rested on that proactive decision to experiment with a new strategy despite the success they had been having. But they only had that opportunity by building a fundamentally sound organization. An organization that was consistently strong, and successful enough to attract a singular talent like Vince Young.

But despite winning at least 10 games per year for 10 years straight in the 2000s, and getting close to the top multiple times during that period, they would win only that one national championship under Mack Brown. And after reaching that ultimate goal, some would say that the Longhorns did indeed become complacent, and that complacency ultimately was the undoing for Mack Brown and a golden era for Texas football. And similarly, Intel never regained the overall market value that they had in 2000, after Andy Grove retired. Apparently Grove was prophetic in saying that "only the paranoid survive".

 Coaching Point – Complacency kills. An asset is only as valuable as our ability and willingness to evolve and improve it.

CHALK TALK

Be proactive.

- **Be Paranoid.** Constantly reexamine your current strengths

- **Keep Exploring.** There may be hidden strengths in your organization that you have not fully exploited.

- **Encourage Experimentation.** Challenge your organization to continuously experiment with new approaches, especially in your core markets.

- **Take Chances.** Great companies are not rash, but they are not afraid to adopt new strategies when the opportunity presents itself

Evaluate Your Assets. Ask yourself:

Value

- Do, or will, customers pay a premium to utilize the asset?

- Does the resource provide a competitive advantage over the competition?

- Does the asset exploit a market opportunity or neutralize an external threat?

Rarity

- Does the resource represent some piece of the value chain that is truly not accessible by other firms?

- Do customers find it unique enough to seek it out without extensive marketing?

Imitability

- What are the cost alternatives for competitors who do not have access to the asset?

- Do customers readily accept alternatives?

- Are there significant patent/IP protections for the resource?

- Is it something you can continue to evolve, or are you relying on legal processes to protect your unique position?

Organizational Fit

- How does the best utilization of the asset fit with your organizational vision and core purpose?

- Does the company have the organizational capability to take advantage of this unique Strength?

Remember, the three axioms of building strategy around unique assets:

- The customer determines value. Make sure you see your resources the way they do.

- A resource is only as strong as your ability to exploit it for tangible value. Be careful about shiny objects.

- Rare and Inimitable resources are rare indeed. Assume you will be copied, and plan accordingly.

STRATEGY: LOOKING EXTERNALLY

The Butler did it

With 1:14 left to go in Super Bowl XLIX, the New England Patriots held a 4 point lead over the Seattle Seahawks. The Seahawks had the ball, but they were still 38 yards away from the touchdown they would need to steal a victory away from the Patriots. On first down, Seahawks quarterback Russell Wilson heaved what amounted to a "jump ball" to wide receiver Jermain Kearse. He took that chance, because Kearse was facing a slightly undersized rookie defensive back named Malcolm Butler, and Wilson liked the matchup. But Butler was in position and disrupted the pass. But as he, Kearse and the ball fell to the ground, the ball bounced off of Kearse's shin, knee, and hand – but not the ground – before Kearse managed to pull in what amounted to as a miracle catch on the Patriots 5 yard line. This was familiar ground for the Patriots, and their coach, Bill Belichick. On two other occasions, the Patriots had lost Super Bowls that they were favored to win, due to improbable, but spectacular catches, by similarly unheralded wide receivers. In what must have felt like déjà vu, the Patriots were now dangerously close to losing their 3rd consecutive Super Bowl, all in dramatic fashion.

AHEAD OF THE CHAINS

After running the ball down to the 1 yard line, the Seahawks lined up with two wide receivers to right side, and sent their top receiver, Doug Baldwin, in motion to the left. That was purposeful, as it forced the Patriots' top cover corner to move to that side of the field to cover him. That left Jermain Kearse and Ricardo Lockette, both big, physical receivers, matched up in 1:1 coverage against the Patriots' defensive backs, that included again, one somewhat undersized rookie in Butler. The play was designed to use that size to their advantage, having Kearse "pick" the inside DB, while Lockette would slide behind him, coming open for a relatively safe and easy throw for Wilson – for a touchdown and a Super Bowl win.

But on the key play, perhaps even more miraculous than Kearse's catch, Butler burst into the middle of the action, and in what seemed like a split second, got in between Lockette and Wilson, and intercepted the pass, sealed the Patriots win, and delivered the Patriots' 4th Super Bowl victory.

Some blamed the Seahawks coach Pete Carroll for what appeared to be an unnecessarily risky play call. But, Carroll got the matchups he wanted, and the play design was perfect for the down, distance, and personnel that he was facing. "I made the decision," said Carroll. "I said, 'Throw the ball.' And unfortunately, the guy makes a great play and jumps in front of the route and makes an incredible play that nobody would ever think he could do." So, in essence, he gave all the credit to Malcolm Butler for defeating a good strategy with a super human performance. But, while Butler had fantastic execution, and made a very athletic play, that wouldn't be telling the whole story

The Patriots were coached by Bill Belichick, who has built his reputation for being an excellent strategist. His strategies are built primarily from careful analysis of his upcoming competition. Before every game, through hours of comprehensive research, he identifies the opportunities and threats that the opponent presents, relative to the capabilities of his team, and prepares strategies to address them. In the week leading up to the Super Bowl, Belichick felt that the biggest threat the Seahawks presented, was the physical matchup of their wide receivers with his defensive backs (future Hall of Famer, Darelle Revis, excluded). One of the plays that most concerned him was the exact formation that the Seahawks presented on that play on the 1 yard line. He replicated it in practice, and repeated it several times, many of which resulted in failures, as Butler was beaten repeatedly. Belichick kept repeating, "When you see them stack the receivers, you have to jump the route. You have to jump the route."

So when Butler saw the formation there on the 1 yard line in the Super Bowl, he didn't deliver a freak athletic play inspired by divine intervention. He executed the play exactly as he was coached. Belichick prepared his team to win, by carefully planning to address the opportunities and threats of the competition. While Belichick is not unique in the concept of building a game plan through film study, he is unique in his willingness to modify his entire offensive or defensive philosophy week to week, depending upon the challenge represented by the competition.

Let's contrast Belichick's strategic perspective with that of Walsh. Walsh had a persistent offensive philosophy that he would apply to every opponent; adding some wrinkles, or minimizing some elements depending upon the opponent, but his core system would never change. From his perspective, success would depend far more on how well his team executed that system, than on different approaches or formations presented by the competition. This assertion is supported by Walsh's approach of scripting the first 15-20 offensive plays of every game. Thus, Walsh represents an excellent example of the "inside-out" approach that characterizes the Resource Model.

The I/O Strategy Model

Belichick, on the other hand, has a new strategy every week. His strategy is based on a careful analysis of the competition and building a plan to exploiting the other team's weakness and/or neutralizing its strengths. As such, Belichick is a classic example of the Industrial Organizational (I/O) Model for Above Average Returns.

The I/O Strategy Model can be characterized as an "outside-in" approach, focusing first on challenges and opportunities outside of the firm, represented by customers, partners and competitors. It is based on a few key assumptions:

- The industry and competitive environment impose pressures and constraints and requires a strategy to overcome them to create above average returns

- Many firms competing in that industry have access to similar resources and thus may pursue similar strategies

- Resources used by firms are highly mobile across firms

Obviously, in football, the "industry" is represented by the sport itself, and the constraints are defined by the rules of the game. Business segments have similar pressures defined the competitive marketplace and customer expectations and constraints defined by regulatory agencies and other structural elements. As for access to resources, the sport of football has very defined rules on the number of players you may have on your team, and in the case of the professional game, even a cap on your total payroll. These guidelines ensure that each team has access to the same type and level of talent. Globalization has created an environment that nearly many resources can be made available to any firm nearly instantaneously, and without undue friction. Finally, there is a convention of "free agency" which creates a very structured approach to creating talent mobility across the NFL. Similarly, a technologically-connected world continues to accelerate the mobility of assets across markets and geographies, so the I/O Strategy for Above

Average Returns is an extremely relevant framework in both modern football and business.

One way in which football is often different than business is the nature of competition. A football team only faces one competitor at a time, which allows teams to prepare very specific strategies for a specific opponent. In the business world that effort would be referred to as competitive analysis – the process of gathering intelligence on other market players, analyzing the data, and developing strategies to compete. In football, the concept of "film study", or how coaches prepare strategy for upcoming opponents, is an excellent metaphor for the I/O model in business.

Let's take a deeper look at Belichick's strategic perspective and how it fits into the SWOT matrix. In preparing to play the Detroit Lions back in 2014, during his film study preparation, Belichick recognized that the strength of the Lions #1 ranked rushing defense was their personnel on the defensive line. Their lineman were huge-bodied run stoppers that clogged gaps very effectively. However, these players were not built for lateral pursuit, and moreover, they were not well-suited to play a lot of snaps in a game due to their obvious bias to size, instead of conditioning. Additionally, their roster was not deep, so, Belichick felt that if he could keep them on the field, and force them to run extensively, he could tire them out, and create opportunities.

During the season, the Patriots had been running the ball nearly 60% of the time. But in this game, they passed on 73% of their plays. They used high-percentage short throws to keep the chains moving; many of them thrown wide to the flats, forced Detroit's lineman to pursue the play laterally. As such, they executed 81 offensive plays, 17 more than the average number that Detroit had been defending that year. Predictably, as the game went on, the Lions defense became less and less effective, and the result was a resounding 34-9 victory for the Patriots.

But in stark contrast, in their game against the Indianapolis Colts the previous week, Belichick had recognized that the opportunity was to run directly at their undersized line. For this game – the only time he employed this strategy for that entire season, he added a 6th offensive lineman on 37 offensive snaps, resulting in a 201 yard rushing performance for unheralded running back, Jonas Gray. Gray played in 7 other games for the Patriots that season, averaging 30yds/game[20]. His performance against the Colts was clearly an Above Average Return, and it was a direct result of an I/O strategy.

	Helpful	Harmful
Internal	**Strengths**	**Weaknesses**
External	**Opportunities**	**Threats**

New England Patriots coach, Bill Belichick epitomizes the Industrial Organization Model, and its more "outside-in" orientation. In this approach, strategy is built by focusing more on the market we choose, or are operating in, and the competition we are facing. If we look at this method through the lens of the SWOT framework, we would be looking outside the firm, identifying opportunities to exploit, or threats to neutralize. Belichick clearly identified an Opportunity with the undersized offensive line of the Colts, and the Threat that the Detroit Lions defensive line represented.

. . . .

[20](Reference, n.d.)

Coaching Point: While you cannot be all things at once, an ability to effectively adapt your game plan to the situation can create competitive advantage.

Analyzing your Customers & Competitors

How are these outside-in strategies developed? They begin with a detailed analysis of the factors that determine success in the external industry environment in conjunction with a realistic comparison of relative competitive strength. For football coaches like Bill Belichick, this analysis is done in the film room, analyzing hours of game film to compare his team to the upcoming game rival in order to identify opportunities to exploit and threats to defend against that can be translated into a winning game strategy. Large business enterprises rely on the strategy function to look outside the organization to identify new business opportunities and situations that represent risk. Because business competition is inherently more complex, this comprehensive process requires gathering and analyzing significant quantitative and qualitative data including market, customer, and competitor research and analysis.

The process involves analyzing customers and major competitors; identifying the key priorities for the customer, and then assessing your company's performance in these areas relative to the competition. This analysis is performed for each major customer or customer segment. Once that is complete, the company will have a clear perspective on their strengths and weaknesses relative to that customer or segment, and also, the biggest opportunities and risks they should pursue and address, relative to their primary competition in that segment. It all begins with a deep and honest assessment of individual customer or customer segment priorities.

In football, the success factors are common to every team; including elements like the size and strength of your lineman, the speed of your running backs, the arm strength of your quarterback, and many others. However, the elements that define success with customers in a competitive marketplace are unique to that market, and to those customers. So, the first step in an effective customer or market analysis must be listing and prioritizing the key aspects that drive their purchase decisions. For a retail business, this might include elements like Price, Assortment, Service Competency, Product Quality, Availability, Distribution Effectiveness, etc. Another key dataset to gather is a realistic assessment of your firm's capabilities relative to those of each of your rivals in each of these key success factors. Since various customer segments or major individual customers have unique sets of needs and priorities, you must gather and organize a separate dataset on each customer or segment that you want to explore.

You can accomplish this in a number of ways. Certainly, you should leverage existing research about your industry that analyzes customer behavior, satisfaction and loyalty, as they will provide objective perspectives on what matters to customers. But that information tends to be very high level, and genericized across too many customer segments to be effective on its own. While external providers can be a valuable part of the process, do not rely solely on research reports and paid analysis. Your first step should be to engage a broad set of your firm's stakeholders in this process that give you a fair and honest assessment of your external environment. Remember your firm's sales team and buyers are constantly interacting in the external environment and have direct insights on how customers and supply chain partners view you versus your competitors. Hopefully, your own people that are closest to the customer can provide you with an accurate assessment of what matters most to your customers and how you stack up versus key rivals. Better yet, you could simply ask your customers directly.

 Coaching Point: Effective use of an "outside-in" strategic approach rests on your ability to accurately gather external insights.

Interpreting Competitive Analysis Data

At this point you have a large amount of data that must be analyzed and interpreted. Organizing the data to effectively interpret it in a way that is useful for generating strategic insights and guiding strategy formulation is a major challenge. A highly effective tool for such interpretation and analysis, used extensively in my strategy consultant practice, is the Customer Analysis Tool (CAT). The tool is used separately for each competitive environment, which might be one key customer, one customer market segment, one product brand, or one geographical area. The level of granularity depends upon the degree of difference in customer needs and priorities and competitive rival overlap across markets.

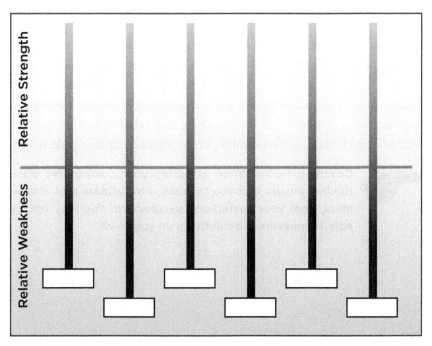

FIGURE 11. THE CAT - CUSTOMER ANALYSIS TOOL

For that unique customer/group of customers and competitor or competitor set, rank each success factor from least important to that customer, to the most important. In the CAT model that would entail writing in those customer priorities in the boxes from left to right, in growing importance to the customer. Once you have the prioritization established, consider each element and evaluate your company's performance on each, from the customer's perspective. For each element, decide if it is an area of strength or weakness for your company, relative to the alternatives on the market. Be honest – the process is only as effective as the analysis you provide. If you are using the CAT, mark your company's performance on the vertical axis over each priority. Needless to say, the further away from the midline, the more pronounced your strength or weakness, relative to market alternatives.

Then, for each priority, repeat that process, but from the perspective of your primary competitor(s). Do you outperform, or underperform in that category, relative to them? Using the CAT, you would plot each competitor's performance on each priority, from the customer's perspective (not yours – this is critical), and relative to your performance in each area. As an example, I have mocked up a sample below.

 Coaching Point: When assessing your competitive positioning, ensure that you take steps to validate that assessment from your customers' perspective. You may not be able to measure it objectively on your own.

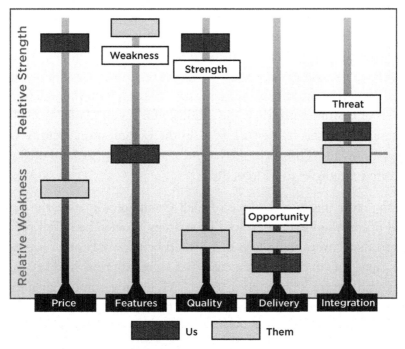

FIGURE 12. CUSTOMER ANALYSIS TOOL EXAMPLE

As you can see, when complete, the CAT shows your data in an interpretable form that is structured to provide strategic insights for competitive advantage. Using this interpreted data can help you identify areas where you may want to focus your resources for maximum return. The figure above is a simulated CAT for a company's performance (noted in blue), compared to a major competitor (noted in green), on a set of purchase criteria for a given customer or segment. Using the given example, we can see that Integration is the most important purchase criteria for this customer. From the plot, you can see that our focus company has a slight edge over the competition on the most important customer priority. As the highest priority for the customer, and only a narrow advantage over the competition, you can easily see that this represents a Threat to the company. This is likely an element that helps define its success in this space, and the competition is nipping at its heels. Conversely, on Delivery, the second priority for the customer, the competition has a slight edge, but neither competitor has distinguished itself. Therefore, this could represent an Opportunity for the company to invest and differentiate, in area that truly matters to the customer. There are other areas of Strength and Weakness, but the further you move to the left on the tool (lower levels of customer priority), the rationale for investment lessens. It is a simple tool and framework to help the organization identify Opportunities and Threats to the business, and to align around the most effective strategies to address them.

Let's revisit the case example of Dell Computers in its early years, and utilize the CAT to explore its strategy. Remember, Dell recognized that government customers could be a key customer segment for them, due to the way that customer segment prioritized key value drivers. One could imagine that the CAT for government customers at that time might have looked something like Figure X.

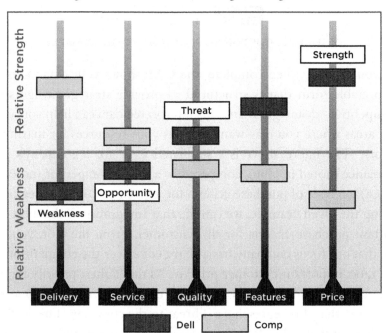

FIGURE 13. CAT EXAMPLE - DELL COMPUTERS AND THE GOVERNMENT CUSTOMER SEGMENT

Obviously, price is going to be a primary value driver for the government sector, and perhaps its highest priority. Dell's low cost structure enabled them to generate margins at a lower sales price point than their rivals, so this was a Strength for them. Another strength was its ability to tailor features to the client need. In this case, this allowed Dell to remove unnecessary features that their government customers did not value, and further extend its price advantage. However, the fixed budget nature of government customers put a value on quality, reliability and service. Dell's competition were large, well-known companies with a perception of good quality, and a field-based service organization. As such, they could discover both threats and opportunities based on quality and service. Creating communication strategies around their solid quality, and deploying innovative service and replacement options can be sources of new value for government customers. Conversely, their lack of inventory, which limited their ability to deliver quickly, was a low priority for government customers, who purchased equipment periodically and predictably, based on annual budgets. That weakness relative to the competition was less relevant due to the low priority that the customer placed on that value driver.

On its own an accumulation of competitive data and customer satisfaction surveys has little benefit to strategy formulation. You need tools like the CAT and other approaches to market analysis to organize and interpret the data in ways that are meaningful for strategy formulation. Consistent mental maps of the competitive landscape, a shared strategic language, and common cognitive assumptions about firm capabilities are essential for formulating aligned strategies across the organization. Aligned strategies complement each other, rather than generating internal strategic competition and external customer confusion. Periodic gatherings of leaders from across the enterprise that represent a broad set of perspectives, organizing them into groups, and using tools like these and facilitated discussion to develop new strategic insights never fails to produce new, actionable, aligned strategic initiatives.

CHALK TALK

Gathering Data on Your Customers and Competitors

- What is your method for assessing your competition?

- How do you ensure you are getting honest and realistic comparisons?

- What matters most to your customers?

- What methods of feedback do you employ to ensure your analysis reflects true customer priorities?

Interpreting Competitive Analysis Data

- How is the competitive analysis data gathered by your firm shared among leaders who create strategy?

- How effective are the tools you use to analyze and interpret the data?

BUILDING STRATEGY BY INTEGRATING INTERNAL AND EXTERNAL INSIGHTS

So we have now examined the concept of strategy, and models for creating Above Average Returns from both internal and external perspectives relative to the firm. And, we have used the SWOT framework as a tool to help us formulate strategy. But how do we pull it all together? How do we determine which is the most meaningful strategy for a particular situation? Again, the game of football provides interesting metaphors on creating strategy out of your SWOT analysis.

Using the SWOT framework as a tool to formulate strategy

I have rearranged the SWOT tool into a 2x2 matrix, graphing Strengths and Weaknesses on one axis and Opportunities and Threats on another. This is similar to the TOWS framework[21], but with some insights gleaned from football.

. . . .
[21](Weihrich, 1982)

	Strengths	Weaknesses
Opportunities	**Offensive Strategies** Use your strength to create change or leverage change to your advantage *Add to your game*	**Tackling Strategies** Actively pursue opportunities to counteract your weakness and change the game *Reinvent the game*
Threats	**Blocking Strategies** Use your strength to block the opportunities of others and maintain the status quo *Make them play your game*	**Defensive Strategies** Identify opportunities to up end the status quo, and create disruption *Change the game entirely*

FIGURE 14. GAME STRATEGY FRAMEWORK

By combining whether you are pursuing either a new Opportunity or mitigating a Risk, and whether you are operating from a position of Strength or Weakness, the model suggests unique strategic approaches for each situation. I will share some examples for each quadrant of this model from the game of football and from the world of business and provide insights on how you might add these strategies to your game.

■ **OFFENSIVE STRATEGIES**

Offensive strategies lie at the intersection of opportunities in the external environment with stronger internal resources than those of rivals. This complementary situation between key competitive success factors and the resources needed to outperform rivals is an ideal environment to formulate strategies that "add to your game".

The Steelers of the 1970's are a case in point. They epitomized fundamental football; lining up with a straightforward strategy, and being successful by simply having better athletes and execution than the opponent. They were essentially following the formula for fundamental football success set by Paul Brown, who mentored their head coach, Chuck Noll. They became a dynasty based on the Steel Curtain defense, and a power running game. Their dominance was punctuated by the fact that the Steelers led the NFL in both rushing and defense in 1976.

But after the 1977 season, the NFL felt that this type of football was not exciting enough for the fans, and wanted to create more opportunities for the offense to score points. Among these changes, they amended the rules on how defenders could make contact with receivers in the passing game. It was meant to help receivers get into their routes more cleanly, and improve their ability to get open more quickly. Ironically, this rule is often referred to as the "Mel Blount Rule", who was a defensive back for the Steelers at the time. He was so dominant, that he was consistently able to physically manhandle opposing receivers, and essentially take them out of the game.

Leveraging Change to Your Advantage

The Steelers knew this rule change was going to open up the passing game, and enable a new level of offense in the NFL. Fortunately, aside from their punishing running game, the Steelers also had a future Hall of Fame quarterback in Terry Bradshaw, and an embarrassment of riches at wide receiver as well, with two future Hall of Famers, Lynn Swann and John Stallworth. Coach Noll quickly ascertained that he was operating from a position of strength, and did not shy away from the opportunity to add to his game, despite having a proven formula for success. In training camp in 1978, he clearly shifted the offensive focus of the Steelers to a much more aggressive approach, emphasizing a vertical passing attack. Despite their transcendent talent, up to that point, neither receiver had ever had over 50 receptions in a season in their entire career. After initiating this offensive strategy, in 1978 and 1979, both receivers increased their production significantly, and both were named All-Pro over those years.

The Steelers used their strength to leverage the change in the rules to their advantage. In so doing, they were able to keep their power running game, but add a powerful passing game. The Steelers' new explosive offense returned them to the Super Bowl for the first time since the 1975 season, and they won their 3rd and 4th Lombardi trophies after the 1978 and 1979 seasons. Those four titles in six years is a level of dominance that has never been repeated before or since. And while they were accomplished with largely the same key personnel, the two pairs of championships were built on two very different offensive strategies.

 Coaching Point: When you are in a position of strength, resist the feeling that change is detrimental. Your strength can enable you to stay on the offensive.

That success was based on organizational leadership that was committed to offensive strategies for finding and exploiting new opportunities, despite a strong incumbent position. There are examples in business as well. VMware is a technology company, now a subsidiary of Dell Technologies that provides cloud and virtualization software and services[22]. VMware built its success on the back of its virtualization technology that enabled more efficient use of server storage. That technology quickly became a standard in the industry, driving step changes in storage efficiency. However, at the height of their success, cloud-based technology was maturing. Instead of simply sticking with a focus on their core business, which played more to their strength, they saw an opportunity to push their own offerings further with cloud-based solutions and services. This somewhat adjacent market represented a risk to their core business, but they decided to stay on the offensive. They embraced the change, at the height of their success, and in so doing, grew the company significantly, and extended their dominant position in the market, longer than if they had stood pat with their existing, successful strategy.

[22](Various, VMware, 2017)

Failing to Leverage Change to Your Advantage

There is a steep price for being timid and failing to stay on the offensive by exploiting new opportunities. For example, while Intel is more commonly known for their Pentium products targeted towards the personal computing platform, they were also actively experimenting in the embedded space (describing the market for processors that powered anything outside computing; segments like networking, automotive, consumer electronics, etc.), where Motorola Semiconductor (later doing business as Freescale and NXP) focused. On more than one occasion, Intel came out with a product that competed directly with one of Motorola Semiconductor's core products. Those products significantly outperformed Motorola's offerings, and at a lower price. Knowing the amount of resources Intel had at their command, Motorola's managers were concerned – alright, petrified, and reasonably so – that Intel may just take over that competitive space. Fortunately for Motorola, Intel almost inexplicably pulled out and sold the product line off to another, far less formidable market player

But the more interesting question is, why would Intel pull out of a space where they clearly had a winning solution? The answer is too much success. During the 2000's, Intel's success with the Pentium product line was at its peak. Volumes were high, as were its gross margins, which were running at roughly 80% - almost unheard of in most manufacturing business models. They had, in hockey parlance, what is known as the "hat trick" (I know this is a football book, but a hat trick is when a hockey player scores three goals in a game) - a leading product that carried a premium price, a market that was booming driving increasing volumes, and an industry-leading manufacturing capability that allowed them to continuously improve costs, yield and quality of production.

 Coaching Point: If you are a market leader, be aware of the tendency to be too conservative, and to ride your incumbent position too long. It can be a recipe for disaster.

So, despite the power of their embedded product offerings, those products would never be able to deliver the kind of margins that the Pentium was delivering. Therefore, at least in the short to medium term, those products would end up being dilutive to their overall gross margins – a key financial metric for the manufacturing and semiconductor industries. If they pursued those embedded solutions, that financially dilutive effect would actually increase as their success and growth in that space increased. Their shareholders, stakeholders that are always more focused on near term returns, might actually be rooting against their success. So, given their status as a public company, and the quarterly expectation of improving margins and returns, they essentially made the choice to abandon any products that would water down the performance of the Pentium product line – which was of course, nearly everything else.

The net result of this disciplined, and perhaps even appropriate behavior, was for Intel to back off from new product categories for an extended period of time. As such, they now find themselves on the outside looking in, on many growing segments in the semiconductor space such as mobile and IoT (Internet of Things), despite having had, at least for a time, perhaps the best talent, IP, and organizational capability in the industry. While their decisions were influenced by financial realities of public companies, many successful companies end up making the same kinds of conservative decisions when they are at their peak of success. And it is that conservatism that ends up speeding the end of their successful run. Sustained success can only be maintained with a consistent offensive game plan.

As a market leader, competitors and new entrants are going to be attracted to compete, enticed by the attractive margins. The more successful you are, the more rapidly the market grows, and the more dynamic the competitive landscape will become. So, appropriately paranoid market-leading business leaders, invest in improving their ability to sense changes in the market and competitive environment.

Then they explore strategic alternatives to apply strengths in new ways to exploit on those opportunities. In other words, they are constantly seeking ways to "Add to Their Game". So, when you are operating from a position of strength, and you changes that threaten your strongest resources, the message here is clear – carefully explore the opportunity to stay on the offensive first.

Coaching Point: If you are participating in a healthy growing market, and you are creating solid profit margins, new entrants will be attracted by them. Plan for it.

There is a defensive tactic used by many football teams when they find themselves in a game in which they are ahead, and feel confident they will win. It is called the "prevent defense", and it essentially means that you are trying to "prevent" the other team from scoring, or at least, scoring too quickly. You instruct your players to play back and allow the other team to make yards, but to at least keep them from scoring too fast. But football players aren't trained to play this way, and it runs counter to their core mindset. Many coaches have blown big leads with this approach, prompting Hall of Fame coach John Madden to say, "the only thing the prevent defense does is prevent you from winning". In business terms, a prevent defense is akin to fighting a rearguard action to maintain the industry environment status quo, slow your rivals down, and hang on to your old strengths longer than the market values them. Be careful not to play "prevent defense" and cost your organization its hard-fought leadership position.

CHALK TALK
OFFENSIVE STRATEGIES

Add to Your Game

- New opportunities will rarely look as good as your current cash cow, but that is not how you should be evaluating it. The question you should ask should be, "Could this opportunity meaningfully add to my game?"

- Many of the strongest opportunities may have significant implications to your current business model. In some cases, it may be better for YOU to cannibalize your existing business, rather than leaving the opportunity to someone else.

- As a market leader, you should be paranoid about that position, and assume that new competitors have you in their gunsights, attracted by the margins you command. Ask yourself, "Can my smaller competitors use this opportunity to their advantage?"

- You should constantly be experimenting with a portfolio of new market opportunities, knowing that not all of them will succeed. Maintaining that portfolio is a required cost of a market leader.

- The most successful organizations proactively look for opportunities, especially when they are at the top of their game, operating from a position of strength. Great business leaders operationalize these types of market sensing capabilities.

▦ DEFENSIVE STRATEGIES

Defensive strategies lie at the intersection of threats in the external environment with weaker internal resources than those of rivals. This confluence of negative situations between key competitive success factors and the resources needed to outperform rivals is an ideal environment to formulate strategies that upend the status quo to "change the game entirely".

While the Steelers were in the midst of a dynasty run at the end of the 1970's, the Baltimore Colts were heading into a tailspin. The Colts had a proud history with several NFL championships, 3 of them led by their hero and face of the franchise, Johnny Unitas (who ironically was from Pittsburgh, and was originally drafted by, and cut by – yes, cut by, the Pittsburgh Steelers). The Colts felt that they had found the heir apparent to Unitas in 1973, drafting Bert Jones out of LSU (and also ironically, from Ruston (LA) High School, the same high school that produced Pittsburgh Steeler quarterback, Terry Bradshaw). Jones had led the Colts to three straight division titles from 1975-77, but unfortunately were knocked out in the first round of the playoffs in each of those years (twice by the Steelers – getting weird now). But Jones sustained some serious injuries, and missed much of the next few years before retiring after the 1982 season. 1977 would be the Colts' last winning season for the next decade, including a winless season in the strike-shortened 1982 season. The once proud franchise had become a laughingstock.

Hope seemed to be arriving in the shape of a young man named John Elway. Elway was an athletic phenomenon coming out of Stanford, and was the consensus #1 pick for the 1983 draft, a pick owned by the Baltimore Colts, due to the winless effort the season before. But the Colts were in such disarray, and so devoid of talent, that Elway assured the Colts that he would never play for them, and would not sign with them if they drafted him. He even threatened that he would drop football altogether and play professional baseball instead (he had been drafted by the Yankees, as a 2-sport marvel) if they ignored his warning and drafted him anyway.

Compounding their problems on the field, the Colts' stadium was the worst in the NFL. They had been arguing with the city of Baltimore and the state of Maryland for the better part of a decade to refurbish it, or to build a new one, without success. On top of its poor condition, the lease agreement they had with the city was financially unfavorable, and the city held the leverage. As such, the ownership group had a failing football team, the available talent had lost faith in their ability to compete, and they did not have the financial resources to invest in turning the situation around. They were not a strong player looking for Opportunities, they were a weak organization surrounded by Threats.

So, instead of an offensive strategy like the Steelers took to add to their game, they needed a defensive strategy. Both Elway and the city of Baltimore held leverage over them, so instead of fighting the competition head on, they needed to change the game altogether. They traded their rights to Elway for a solid quarterback – stabilizing a position of need - and future draft picks. In so doing, they were utilizing two tenets of Defensive strategies – not being afraid to fold a bad hand, and instead, focusing on a longer term win, instead of insisting on a complete win today.

By trading Elway, they avoided the complete disaster of receiving nothing in return for #1 pick in the draft, and the most heralded, can't-miss player in recent history. When you are truly in an untenable position, playing a defensive strategy of recovering whatever value is available, despite pride or decision anchoring. Playing from a position of weakness, you are not often going to win games of brinksmanship. Think instead of how to pivot, prevent further damage, and try to find sources of future value. Their resolution solved an immediate need –

a viable starting quarterback for the upcoming season, and new draft picks to help them live to fight another day.

 Coaching Point: When faced with an unwinnable hand, find ways to compromise, to limit damage, and create future opportunities.

The Colts still needed to address their financial position. They negotiated with the league to be involved in an upcoming NFL expansion, and took the opportunity to move the team out of Baltimore. It was a move no one expected – or saw for that matter, since they packed up the facility and moved the team to Indianapolis in the middle of the night. In so doing, they modeled another key defensive strategy – questioning accepted truths.

League expansions are typically just that – expanding the league by creating new teams that establish themselves in new cities that currently do not have teams. It had not generally been a venue for existing teams to relocate. The accepted axiom for NFL franchises in the modern era had been that teams were essentially "married" to their cities. But the Colts ownership challenged that truth and convinced the league to allow them to become an "expansion" franchise in Indianapolis, leaving Baltimore – a tradition-rich football city – without an NFL team. In so doing, they changed their financial position entirely, by changing the game.

Coaching Point: Successful Defensive strategies often begin by questioning and challenging accepted "truths", and to make abrupt moves to change the game.

A decade or so later, now financially sound, they hired proven General Manager Bill Polian who built an excellent foundation of talent, starting with Peyton Manning, who became the new face of the franchise in Indianapolis. They also hired Tony Dungy as head coach (a former Steeler, wow this is weird), who gave the team a winning culture, and its first championship since Johnny Unitas.

Changing the Game Altogether

There have been several popularized examples of struggling companies that have fought off threats from a position of weakness, and it nearly always is credited to a strategy to completely change the game. One popular example is about Steve Jobs. After a meteoric rise to the top of the personal computing industry, Apple had some missteps in executing new product releases, and by the mid 1980's, the company was floundering. In a well-documented clash with the company's CEO and board of directors, Jobs found himself looking for a new challenge after being fired by the company that he himself had founded.

While he was still at Apple, he often met with academic customers, and several had shared their need for a more powerful computer workstation to power certain calculation-heavy applications. So, after leaving Apple, he started Next Computer in 1985 to fill that need. By the early 90's it was obvious that the workstations were never going to succeed in the market, and investors had poured in well over $100M into Next. Running out cash and options, Jobs had to question accepted realities, and try to change the game entirely. He questioned whether Next had to actually be a hardware company. Taking the innovative software IP they had created for the workstations, Jobs repositioned Next as a software company.

Doing that was going to require focus. Organizations operating from a position of weakness like Next cannot afford a broad focus. So, he had to make the hard decision to trim a significant amount of the workforce and focus the rest on the new software platform. He did not have the luxury to trying to balance alternatives. To be successful in changing the game, he was going to have to go "all in".

Coaching Point: When operating from a disadvantaged position, you must be deliberate. When you find an opportunity to change the game, you must focus your resources to succeed.

But working from a position of weakness, you often cannot change the game on your own – you need to look at customers, competitors, and unlikely partners. Jobs knew that Apple was going to need an operating system for their next generation products and that they didn't have an answer. So, instead of continuing to pursue a losing proposition as a hardware company, he redirected the company's resources towards building the software IP that would make him an attractive acquisition for Apple. It wasn't as immediate of a move as it may seem in retrospect. Jobs had to commit these software resources to create a completely new platform that would unlock the functionality and feature opportunities he knew that his customers were going to want.

He was successful, and ultimately sold Next to Apple for $429M in cash and stock. In one end run, he made solid returns for shareholders, including himself, and regained his position as CEO of Apple. Moreover, he reshaped his relationship with Bill Gates and Microsoft. Jobs had seen Gates as a hated rival throughout most of Apple's early successful run, as they both invested in aggressively competing platforms. Knowing that he needed capital to keep Apple solvent, he reached out to Gates, and made a surprising cross-licensing agreement in exchange for a $150M investment in Apple by Microsoft[23]. But the underlying change in his thinking is the point here. Jobs was quoted as saying, "we have to let go of this notion that for Apple to win, Microsoft has to lose." Leaders that are successful winning with defensive strategies, must change the game entirely, and that always begins with changing one's perspective.

 Coaching Point: Changing the game from a completely defensive position often requires creating new partnerships, perhaps from unlikely parties, to create opportunities out of threats.

. . . .
[23](Heisler, 2014)

CHALK TALK
DEFENSIVE STRATEGIES

Change the Game Altogether

Identify opportunities to up end the status quo, and create disruption. Question every accepted "truth" about the market you are in

- "What if that "truth" wasn't true? How can you turn it upside down?

- Innovate to redefine the business model in the industry – or your role in that industry

When you are in a position of weakness, you may not be in a position to win today, but how do you position yourself to win tomorrow?

- Focus on the long game instead of chasing a strategy that will only just get you out of last place. Next to last is still not winning.

- Imagine what the Desired Future State is, and start working towards that, not some incremental position just above terrible.

When you are in a position of weakness, you cannot spread yourself too thin

- What areas of the business can you trim off that will allow you to put more of your resources behind your best bet for success?

- You can't outrun a bad balance sheet. The perfect time to absorb losses is when you are already down. Clean up nagging issues, and take on the tough decisions that are holding you back, now.

Look at your situation from the other side of the looking glass

- What are your attractive assets? What competitor they be most attractive to? What value do those assets have for your competition? You may be more valuable than you think, to the right market player.

- Consider your largest customers. Would any of them find value in vertically integrating your product or service into their offering – either from a cost reduction aspect, or a great value to their customers?

Recognize the situation for what it is

- Be conservative with your cash until you find your best move

- Don't get too optimistic. Don't be afraid to fold a bad hand. You and your investors can live to fight another day.

▪ TACKLING STRATEGIES

Tackling strategies lie at the intersection of opportunities in the external environment with weaker internal resources than rivals. This mismatch situation between key competitive success factors and the resources needed to outperform rivals is an ideal environment to formulate strategies that "reinvent the game".

Like defensive strategies, those in this quadrant often require a fresh perspective. Sometimes the change in perspective that you need is about the customers or markets you pursue. Organizations that are operating from a weak position need to reexamine who their customer base is, or could be. Often, one of the fastest and most reliable methods for doing so, is to identify a set of customers that have been disenfranchised by the market leaders. Going back to our example about the Baltimore Colts leaving Baltimore, you can imagine Baltimore fans became a disenfranchised customer group, both literally and figuratively.

Well, the Cleveland Browns found themselves in an eerily similar situation as the Colts had experienced, roughly 10 years later[24]. When evaluating alternatives, Browns owner Art Modell knew that fans in Baltimore had been a diehard football city for decades, and were likely desperate for a team to follow. So, when he made the call to move the team out of Cleveland, he chose Baltimore as the new location for his franchise.

With better resources and a new, engaged fan base, Modell made the investments necessary for a successful franchise. He rebranded the team as the Ravens that made the team feel new, especially to his new base of fans there in Baltimore. To do so, he engaged the local fans to participate in creating the brand. Telephone surveys, focus groups and public events were all used to bring the local fans into the process of defining the identity of the new franchise, including the name, logo, colors, etc. Since the move, the Ravens have been a very successful franchise, reaching the playoffs consistently, and winning two Super Bowls.

 Coaching Point: You can often find a way to reinvent the game by finding disenfranchised groups that have been overlooked or treated poorly by market leaders or competitors in incumbent positions.

This is a proven approach for troubled companies as well. In 2011, T-Mobile USA was owned by Deutsche Telecom, a large German telecommunications conglomerate. T-Mobile had been languishing as a mainstream competitor, running 4th in a four team race. AT&T attempted to buy T-Mobile, primarily for access to its wireless spectrum rights. The acquisition seemed like a natural strategic move for AT&T, but later that year, facing heavy antitrust resistance from the FCC, AT&T was forced to abandon the acquisition[25]. This left

. . . .
[24](Various, Cleveland Browns relocation controversy, n.d.)
[25](De La Merced, 2011)

T-Mobile in an even worse position. During the period before and during the failed acquisition process, they had focused on shedding cost, not on attracting and retaining customers, since they were a target for their assets, not their robust customer base. Moreover, the failed acquisition further reinforced to the market that they were not a real player in the market, and they were left in disarray. Essentially, a quick assessment of their position would show that they had a strong portfolio of wireless spectrum, $4B in cash from the breakup fee from AT&T, a weak and tarnished brand, and essentially, no customers. Gordon Gekko would have clearly chopped it up and sold it in pieces in a corporate raid.

Actually, pursuing a quick exit to reclaim shareholder value in a situation like this would be not be a crazy idea. But T-Mobile took a different tack. Instead, they reinvented the game. They had a strong set of assets – what they were missing were customers, and a brand that customers could believe in. So, instead of folding up shop, they performed an exhaustive analysis on mobile access consumers. They went in pursuit of insights that might provide opportunities that they could exploit to reinvent the game, instead of playing the one the market leaders were playing.

What they found may not seem surprising. Everyone hated their wireless carrier, even those using the two market leaders, AT&T and Verizon. Despite their clear market leadership in nearly every aspect of the customer experience, mobile phones are just simply not as reliable as the historic POTS platform (Plain Old Telephone Service). And, as a very complex technology solution, the service was subject to both handset and backend infrastructure glitches and call drops. That combined with a seemingly constant escalation of overall cost and fees of every type, left many consumers unhappy. Surprisingly, they found that none of that negative energy was directed at the handset maker, only the access provider. From the consumer's perspective,

Apple made cool technology, but AT&T and Verizon were insensitive and ineffective jerks. They were just necessary jerks, which made the perception from customers that much worse.

So, that created an opening for T-Mobile. Consumers felt that AT&T and Verizon "nickel-and-dimed" them – T-Mobile would have one price that included everything. They charged you for data overages – T-Mobile's plan would be "all-you-can-eat". Bills from both of the market-leading companies were complicated and littered with lines and lines of fees that baffled the reader – T-Mobile would simplify that. In so doing, they redefined the battle lines in the wireless space. The two market leaders ran very similar marketing strategies that consisted to new recipes of the same ingredients – certain amount of minutes and data for a given price. T-Mobile's approach destroyed that set of rules, and redefined the dashboard that formed the basis of the wireless market.

 Coaching Point: Successful Tackling strategies often redefine common battle lines that define the incumbent position, and allow players coming from a weaker position to create new opportunities.

But, just a different billing strategy would not be enough to enable them to reinvent the game. They would have to have a fresh approach for everything that frustrated the customers of the market leaders, and make it easy for them to switch. They would reinvent the customer experience and brand themselves as the "un-carrier" – embodying the opposite of everything the market leaders represented. By taking this approach, they turned their pricing strategy and their brand into a movement. T-Mobile and its customers would be the "Us", pitted against "Them" – the major carriers, who would be cast as the "bad guys".

Coaching Point: To truly reinvent the game, you will likely have go beyond traditional price-value marketing strategies, and engage your customers emotionally. To turn customers away from market leaders, you may need to create a "movement", not a promotion.

They didn't have the retail footprint or huge staff of software engineers to make T-Mobile-specific apps and value-add software, so they partnered for both, delivering important capabilities and features at a far lower cost. They brought in some key talent from the majors, to help them address some critical technology roles. And they spent aggressively, but surgically, on the marketing they would need to reshape their brand, and win new subscribers.

Well, the strategy worked[26], and the results have been staggering. Once at death's door, as of Q1 2017, T-Mobile was the fastest growing major wireless carrier in the world. And a meaningful portion of that growth is at the expense of the market leaders. It added over 1 million net new subscribers in Q1 2017, while both AT&T and Verizon lost subscribers[27]. It recorded double digit improvements in revenue in 2016, and nearly doubled net income over the year before. The "un-carrier" was able to pivot from a position of weakness to one of strength from their willingness to be bold in the face of risk, exploit opportunities, and reinvent the game.

. . . .

[26](Schlappig, 2016)
[27](Jhonsa, 2017)

CHALK TALK
TACKLING STRATEGIES

Reinvent the Game

Identify opportunities to redefine the competitive battle lines

- Where do the market leaders dissatisfy the customer base? How can you take advantage of that?

- What metrics are not being discussed? How can you establish a brand identity based on a different dashboard?

Invest surgically on your Opportunity

- When you identify your point of differentiation, focus your resources in truly separating from the pack

- Identify the customer segment that will be most attractive to that point of differentiation, and pursue them aggressively

- Create a brand identity that clearly highlights your opportunity

You will need new stakeholders to support your initiative

- Enlist customers into your "movement". Many consumers like to be with the underdog, so make them feel like they are part of the team

- Top heavy markets disenfranchise many market players. Look for opportunities to partner.

- You will need top talent to be successful. Over-invest in key talent by poaching a few star performers from the market leaders. They will be a + in your column, and a − in theirs.

■ BLOCKING STRATEGIES

Blocking strategies lie at the intersection of threats in the external environment with stronger internal resources than those of rivals. This mismatch situation between key competitive success factors and the resources needed to outperform rivals is an ideal environment to formulate strategies that "make them play your game".

The Alabama Crimson Tide in 2017 are in a very different place from the Cleveland Browns in 1999, or T-Mobile in 2011, for that matter. As such, they need a very different strategy.

The University of Alabama has long been considered one of college football's elite programs. Once coached by the legendary Bear Bryant, they are now led by Nick Saban, who is creating a legend of his own. The Tide have become a dynasty in a sport that has not had a true dynasty for decades; winning four national championships since the 2009 season. No other program has one more than 3, even going back nearly 50 years.

Alabama employs traditional offensive and defensive philosophies, much like Steelers of the 1970's, and for the same reason. Those approaches are tremendously effective when you have superior talent. Those philosophies are built on power, and they encourage the opponent to line up and match up with you head to head. So, with superior talent, you will win those battles more often than not, and therefore, you will likely win the war.

Coaches with teams of weaker talent can't employ these traditional strategies very effectively. Their strategies are likely to be defensive, i.e. designed to change the game. They have to stretch every rule and use other tactics to unbalance the opponent, like surprise personnel substitutions and calling plays in a very short time frame. Their offenses such as the West Coast, the Spread, or even versions of the triple option like the Wishbone, are designed to do just the opposite of Alabama's more traditional offense. They avoid man-on-man matchups and succeed by misdirection or by creating mismatches in non-traditional ways.

Consistent with his position of Strength, and facing Threats to that market leadership, Saban has employed common blocking strategies. The Alabama coach sees these innovations for what they are – strategies to change the game to reduce his competitive advantage. And as a market leader, he knows that he must use his position of strength to limit the impact of those innovations. One way is through regulation. Saban has consistently attacked many of these tactics and innovations, even labeling some as "unsafe", and pursued rule changes to limit them or eliminate them altogether[28]. The goal of blocking strategies like this is to make the opponent play your game.

Lock Them Out

Companies that are market leaders take similar strategies. The external affairs function of large enterprises are essentially lobbyists operating within the firm. They are in place to influence legislation and regulation towards the concerned interests of the company. As leaders they tend to be larger companies with incumbent positions that can be put at risk by legislation or regulation, so they will spend significant amounts of money to influence it. The recent case example around the telecommunications industry is a perfect example of companies with extensive external affairs operations that are attempting to ensure that laws and regulations adapt to their business model, not the other way around.

Another recent and public example is the taxi industry. Uber, Lyft, and the multitude of other players in the ride-hailing industry have introduced massive disruption to the taxi business, which is built on the asset of the "medallion". Medallions refer to a licensing process

. . . .
[28](Cooper, 2014)

that defines and limits the amount of legal taxi cabs available in a certain geography. Those medallions are owned by private companies, and are very costly, as one might expect from a license that provides you a ticket to a monopoly or oligopoly of a given market. So, ride-sharing businesses represent a massive threat to that once strong market position. They essentially side-step the licensing process altogether, reinventing the game, from a position of weakness.

So, naturally taxi companies would pursue blocking strategies. In 2016, in my home city of Austin, taxi companies were successful in getting legislation passed that would force ride-hailing companies to be subject to the same type of ordinances and regulation that they are. Uber and Lyft argued that they were technology companies that connected drivers to riders, not a transportation company, in a traditional sense, and therefore should not be party to those same requirements. When they lost that argument, they exited the market, rather than comply.

 Coaching Point: If you are in a market-leading or financially-advantaged position, use your resources to influence regulatory bodies or industry groups to block reinvention strategies.

Meanwhile, they were already lobbying the state of Texas to get a state law passed that was more advantageous to them, and could prevent them from having to argue the same case in cities all over the state. The disrupter has now become the de facto market leader, and they are employing blocking strategies of their own. They were successful, and have now reentered the Austin market, and have a stateside decision that will allow them to defend their franchise and business model across the state, circumventing any annoying city ordinances.

Starve Them Out

Football offers other unique insights to successful Blocking strategies. Consider the recruiting of high school athletes. Back in the

60's and 70's, the Texas Longhorns were experiencing a long run of success, and cemented their position as one of the elite programs in the country. Being situated in the state of Texas was a key strategic advantage; one of, if not the biggest incubators of football talent in the country. Much of that talent grew up wanting to be a Longhorn someday, so the University of Texas could pick and choose the best of the best. But they did more than that. Being one of the largest and most well-funded universities in the country, coupled with support from oil-rich alumni donors, the athletic program had almost unlimited resources. Moreover, at that time, there was no restriction as to the number of scholarship athletes a program could have. As such, Darrell Royal used those resources to grant scholarships to any and all top athletes he wanted. He provided scholarships to athletes that he sometimes knew would likely never start for his football team. But he did so, to ensure that no other program would have them, and use them against him.

In 1973, Title IX rules were passed that among other things, limited the number of scholarships a college program could offer. It had a profound impact on elite programs like Texas, who could no longer play "keep away" with the best athletes across the state. Darrell Royal retired after the 1976 season, his first non-winning season in his 20 year career as the head coach of the University of Texas. As a market leader, hoarding talent is an important blocking strategy.

IBM was successful with talent hoarding strategies in the early days of computing. There was a scarcity of talent in computing systems at that time, and they knew competition was coming. But they extended their near ownership of the space by a decade or more by hoarding all of the eligible talent in the industry, and blocking upstarts from getting the critical mass of talent they would need to reasonably compete with them.

Coaching Point: Companies that are trying to reinvent the game, or to change it entirely, still need experienced talent. As a market leader, it is critical that you hold onto your key talent. Do what you have to do to keep them, as it denies upstarts from the resources they will need to disrupt you.

Upstarts need talent, but they also need cash. Disruptive companies often establish a beachhead in a specific area of expertise that represents a threat to the incumbent. They need that beachhead to not only establish their legitimacy, but also to create a cash flow to finance their growth and expansion. Market leaders will often make efforts to block that cash flow by any means necessary. Back in the 90's, at the outset of the internet age, Netscape created the first modern web browser, and it quickly grew to be the industry standard. Microsoft was initially slow to embrace the importance of the internet, but once they saw its significance, they recognized that Netscape and their browser technology as a major threat to their ownership of the personal computing "desktop", and also their growing business around servers. So, instead of slugging it out with Netscape to see who would win the commercialization of the browser business, they just gave it away. They built it into every product for free, and even installed it into the very fabric of their ubiquitous operating system, rendering Netscape's first mover advantage inert, by using their own largesse as their blocking strategy.

 Coaching Point: Upstarts need cash to fund their disruptive efforts. Give away products or "buy" strategic business opportunities if you have to. If you don't block their small wins, they may turn into bigger ones that you can no longer block.

Blocking strategies are about using your size to your best advantage. As a market leader, you have the resources to employ a wide range of tactics to control the competition and make them play your game.

CHALK TALK
BLOCKING STRATEGIES

Make Them Play Your Game

Hoard Talent

- Who are the key people in your organization that could really make a difference if they worked for new market entrants? Lock these people up in contracts or reward them with compensation packages that new entrants cannot match.

- What are the key sources of talent in the industry? How can you create a commanding presence in those venues to ensure you get the best of the best?

Upstarts need cash to survive, so cut off their supply

- New entrants are smaller companies, and even small wins can be helpful to them. Leaders often overlook these opportunities, so set up approaches to see that you don't.

- When competing directly with threatening new entrants, "buy" the deals if you have to. The small dilution in your margins will hurt you far less than it will hurt them.

Market leaders are big enough to influence regulatory and legislative resources, new entrants are not.

- Use your resources to employ lobbyists on your behalf

- Advertising is expensive, so use it to your advantage. Keep the focus on the metrics that you control

GAME PLAN
STRATEGY

In this section, we have discussed how companies have used strategy as a way to deliver Above Average Returns. To create an effective strategy for your organization, you are going to have to look at your organization from both the inside-out, and from the outside-in. You can refer to the two models that we explored in this section:

- **The Resource Model of Above Average Returns**

  > Each firm is defined by its unique collection resources and capabilities, which provide the basis of its strategy, and ultimately determine the return they will generate

  > Firms collect different resources and assets over time, and thus develop their own unique approach or strategy to create competitive advantage

  > Resources may not be highly mobile across firms

- **The Industrial Organizational (I/O) Model of Above Average Returns**

  > The industry and competitive environment impose pressures and constraints and requires a strategy to overcome them to create above average returns

  > Many firms competing in that industry have access to similar resources and thus may pursue similar strategies

  > Resources used by firms are highly mobile across firms

PRE-GAME

While the two models are described as two unique, or even perhaps competing models, you should consider them both, as opportunities to look at your organization from different perspectives. However, you should consider the nuances inherent in the models as described by the bulleted statements above. Consider the following questions:

- Which aspect of your environment seems to most significantly impact how organizations behave in your space, the unique assets and resources they have acquired, or the customers or the dynamics of the industry?

- Do more than one of the major players in the market take on very similar strategies, or by nature do they all have unique approaches to creating returns for stakeholders?

- Do resources move readily across market players, or is movement restricted by patent, regulation or other market forces?

The answer to these three questions will provide insight into which of these models may have the most to offer you in your strategy development process.

- **Ensure you have a clear vision.** Remember, you cannot create a strategy towards an undefined destination.

  > **Key Play:** Use the tools in the Vision section of this book to create a clear and vivid picture of your Desired Future State. Ensure that you have set tangible goals that you are aiming towards. The fuzzier the goal, the more difficult it is to create a strategy to get there.

- **Identify a comprehensive set of your external stakeholders.** Don't just stop at customers and shareholders.

  > **Key Play:** Consider all of the partners, associations, concern groups, supporters, opponents, competitors, etc. that all have a stake in seeing you win or lose. Clarify their relationship to you, and how they benefit when you either succeed or fail.

- **Pull your numbers together.** Engage your sales, supply chain and finance teams to pull together an exhaustive set of data. Strategic decisions must be built on data.

> **Key Play:** Consider all of the partners, associations, concern groups, supporters, opponents, competitors, etc. that all have a stake in seeing you win or lose. Clarify their relationship to you, and how they benefit when you either succeed or fail.

GAME TIME

- **Assess your current position.** Are you in a position of strength or weakness?

  > **Key Play:** Certainly, any assessment of your competitive position would include gathering relevant market data from industry analysts to get a grounding in objective data. But your analysis would not be complete without first hand interaction with customers to help you create an honest and realistic first assessment of your strategic position. Utilize the CAT to create or validate your understanding of how your customers prioritize your capabilities and value elements, and how you stack up against the competition on those elements. You need to engage your go-to-market organization in the same exercise; either in addition to customers, or in lieu of direct feedback.

- **Compile a comprehensive list of your internal assets and resources.** It is more than just plant, property and equipment.

  > **Key Play:** Consider employees and which ones you cannot live without. Catalogue your technology patents, and any technical assets that are unique to the market. Utilize the VRIO model to validate whether your assets are strong enough to build a strategy around.

- **Choose your strategy.** Once you have a firm handle on your desired goal, the assets you will use to reach them, and the relative strength of your position, then you can choose a winning strategy.

> **Key Play:** When you are struggling to come up with an overarching strategy that defines your organization, sometimes it is more efficient to build the strategy from the ground up, instead of the top-down. Gather your team together, and organize them in small groups. Give each group a specific goal, and arm them with the output of the work that was done around assessing your assets and your competitive position. Provide them with the Game Strategy Framework, and have them develop strategic "plays" that are consistent with the quadrant they are working in. It is best practice to have at least two groups attacking the same issue so that you generate a range of approaches to choose from. This is a complex activity that is often best performed with an experienced facilitator.

POST-GAME

- **Keep it Simple, Stupid.** Strategy is a heady topic, and the more complex it sounds, the less people believe it, or know how to execute it. The most elegant strategies are the ones that anyone can understand, and can be shared without a long narrative down a winding road.

  > **Key Play:** Work on your strategy communication statements. At its core, any clear strategy has three working elements; a goal, an asset or capability, and a stakeholder. "We are going to grow revenue faster than the market, through incremental sales of our services package to existing customers." This is the essence of strategy, and as a leader, creating clarity of direction is one of your most important jobs. So, invest the time to ensure you can make your strategy short, simple, and clear.

- **Strategy is about what you DON'T do, too.** Michael Porter once said, "The essence of strategy is choosing what not to do". In my engagements with clients, it is common to hear leaders at the front line and mid-level comment that they feel their company "doesn't have a strategy". That perception arises from two primary causes – that there is no communication or discernible direction for the organization, or, perhaps even common, that the organization seems to pursue everything. Sometimes the most effective communication of strategy is message that is sent when the organization chooses not to pursue a particular approach.

> **Key Play:** Once you have your strategy statements crafted, examine your current customer roster and revenue streams. Consider whether those customers, assets, or methods are consistent with your stated direction. If not, give serious consideration to discontinuing. Just like that sense of relief you feel after cleaning out a closet, or having a garage sale, your people will feel a weight lifted from them when you have the will to walk away from efforts that are not consistent with your strategy.

- **You think you have a strategy – prove it.** "Strategy is resource allocation. When you strip away all of the noise, that's what it comes down to." Jack Welch. So, if you think you have a strategy, test it by seeing how you actually allocate resources, and see if it matches up with your statement. If you are a football coach, and you say you value special teams, check your practice schedule, and see how much practice time you actually commit to it. But if you are a business leader, see where you put your people and how you spend your capital.

> **Key Play:** Either through HR, or by just laying out your own organization, see where your headcount resides. How many people and how much payroll do you have committed to which groups and functions. Does it reflect what you communicate as your strategic intent?

> **Key Play:** Moreover, make a list of your "A" players. Where in the organization are they located? Do you have star players in key positions? If you were starting with a blank sheet of paper, and were going to allocate a scarce number of top talent people across your organization, where would you put them? Where would they have the most leverage? Comparing that plan with what you currently have, is the essence of a basic talent strategy.

> **Key Play:** Look at your balance sheet and your income statement, or simply how you spend money in your organization. Where do you put your scarce capital? What are the biggest drivers of expenses in the business? Do those expenditures directly and tangibly correlate to advancing your strategic vision, or do they create revenue from your strategic assets and customers. If not, seriously consider aligning them. Fundamentally sound organizations put their money where their mouth is – or in this case, allocate resources in a way that matches the strategy statements they make to their organizations and to the external market

- **Again, Keep Score.** The goals you set that define your Strategic will cease to matter unless you report your progress. The only reason for a strategy is to generate a return that you would not otherwise get without it. If you are not getting the results you are looking for, perhaps you have the wrong strategy.

> **Key Play:** Conduct and annual review of your strategies. This is a critical effort for you and your organization, and should always be done before setting goals for the next year. There is no greater crime from a leader, than having them send their people into losing battles that they had no real chance of winning. Putting your people and capital in a position where they can generate an above average return is your role as a strategic leader. So, periodically, you need to critically evaluate your return on strategy.

Strengths	Weaknesses
Offensive Strategies	**Tackling Strategies**
Use your strength to create change or leverage change to your advantage	Actively pursue opportunities to counteract your weakness and change the game
• Use your extensive resources to continuously scan the market landscape for new opportunities	• Look for opportunities to redefine competitive battle lines – attack the metrics and frameworks that define the market today
• Engage the organization on how to translate that change into new ways to add to your game	• Identify specific customer segments that are dissatisfied with the market leaders
• Experiment with new opportunities regularly. While many new ventures will often not represent an opportunity of a meaningful size, they provide a portfolio of projects that will produce the large businesses of tomorrow.	• Focus investment narrowly on addressing key segments and unique customer problems
	• Ensure that your branding focuses on your differentiation from market leaders – position yourself as the agent of change
• When facing disruptive opportunities, consider cannibalizing your own business before allowing competitors to do it for you	• Utilize emotional elements to translate your brand from a simple product or service into a "movement" that customers can join in with you
• Be paranoid. Anticipate competitive threats.	• Poach key talent away from market leaders to build your expertise
• Don't get complacent. Stay on the offensive.	• Be tenacious.
Add to your game	*Reinvent the game*

(left vertical label: Opportunities)

135

Strengths	Weaknesses
Blocking Strategies	**Defensive Strategies**
Use your strength to block the opportunities of others and maintain the status quo	Identify opportunities to up end the status quo, and create disruption
• Use largesse to starve out the competition – "buy" the business or give away what they want to sell	• Question all accepted "truths"
	• Your goal is to disrupt the industry or to radically redefine your role in that industry
• Hoard Talent – retain your top talent at all costs as they can lend legitimacy to new entrants	• You may not want to try for an all-out win in one stroke – take approaches that allow you to keep fighting while building long-term capability
• Use resources to shape regulatory policy to your advantage	
• Block alliances that threaten your leadership position	• Focus your resources, both financial and human on your key strategy – you cannot afford to spread yourself too thin
• Don't underestimate smaller players – they can grow into competitors that will be far more expensive to defend against, than they are to buy or kill today	• Take on the difficult decisions now – it is the time to look at your situation objectively and honestly
• Encourage and challenge smaller competitors to compete on your terms – make them play your game	• Engage with customers that are disenfranchised by the market leaders
• Be aggressive with competition	• Look for unusual partnership opportunities – with suppliers, customers and even competitors which might be able to make your assets more valuable or accessible to another market
	• Avoid strategies that simply delay the inevitable – you must change the game entirely
	• Be practical
Make them play your game	*Change the game entirely*

The word "Threats" appears vertically along the left side of the table.

FIGURE 15. DETAILED GAME STRATEGY FRAMEWORK

SECTION III
CULTURE-
SUPPORTING YOUR SYSTEM

DESIGNING YOUR CULTURE

The Ohio State Buckeyes capped their 2014 season by celebrating a national championship in their win over Oregon. That win was not as surprising as their win in the playoff against the favored, and seemingly unbeatable, Alabama Crimson Tide. But neither victory was as improbable as the fact that the Buckeyes were in position for a championship at all. Prior to the season, two-time Big Ten Offensive player of the year, and Heisman Trophy candidate quarterback, Braxton Miller, was injured in practice. With Miller requiring surgery and lost for the season, head coach Urban Meyer was forced to turn to an unproven redshirt freshman, J.T. Barrett. Barrett struggled early, but found his rhythm along the way, and again, the Buckeyes seemed in position to compete for a title. That was until Barrett was also lost for the season due to injury in the final regular season game against Michigan. Now, to claim that national title, Ohio State was going to have to win the Big Ten Championship Game, a College Football Playoff semifinal game, and the National Championship, with their 3rd string quarterback, Cardale Jones.

Of course, the Buckeyes did click off those three victories, and did go on to claim that championship trophy, despite the adversity they faced. I believe that if you asked Urban Meyer how they were able to perform such a feat, I think he would sum it up in one word; Alignment.

Alignment reflects his philosophy for a winning organizational culture for his football teams. It provides clarity on the behaviors he expects from his players and their responsibilities to each other, and how that instills toughness and resiliency into his teams. And that toughness and resiliency was what enabled them to win the national championship, despite the adversity they faced that year. But Meyer has been successful everywhere he has been – leading Bowling Green to bowl games, Utah to an undefeated season, and both Florida and Ohio State to national championships[29]. During that run, he has hired a broad array of assistant coaches, and has employed several different offensive and defensive systems. The one common element that spans his coaching career has been his approach to building a championship organizational culture.

So, what exactly is organizational culture? According to Meyer, "Culture is what we believe, how we behave, and the experience that our behavior produces for each other[30]." Sometimes that culture is carefully cultivated, like the ones that Meyer created at his various coaching stops. Sometimes it emerges over time, as an organization grows and evolves. But whether intentional or accidental, every organization has a culture. And Meyer knew that having an effective culture makes the difference between winning and losing - "Strategy determines scheme and technique. Culture determines attitude and effort." His coaching record bears that out.

Culture Eats Strategy for Breakfast

Research in the corporate environment resoundingly supports this belief as well. Harvard professor, John Kotter studied over 200 companies, comparing their performance over time and objective measurements of their organizational culture[31]. The results were astound-

[29](Various, Urban Meyer, n.d.)
[30](Meyer U. , 2015)
[31](Kotter & Heskett, 1992)

ing. Over a ten year period, firms with effective cultures grew revenue 5 times faster than those that did not. Other comparisons were even more profound; firms with effective cultures grew their net profit more than 700% over that period, compared to essentially no growth for companies with relatively ineffective cultures, and their stock performed 12 times better. The data is overwhelming. As management guru Peter Drucker is often quoted to have said, "Culture Eats Strategy for Breakfast."

So what is an effective culture? Is there one perfect culture that would be appropriate for every organization? Clearly that is not the case, or it would have been bottled and sold by now. By examining some of the examples of leaders and organizations we have discussed so far – Mack Brown and his Texas Longhorn teams, Bill Walsh's San Francisco 49ers, Bill Belichick's New England Patriots, and Urban Meyer's Ohio State Buckeyes – we can see that they each had their own leadership style, and all created unique cultures, within very similar environments and competitive landscapes, and yet all were successful. So, what can we learn from each of these successful leaders and the organizational cultures they created? What unique attributes did they focus on that fueled their success?

ORGANIZATIONAL CULTURE ARCHETYPES

▓ ONE-NESS

So, let's start with Urban Meyer, and his focus on Alignment. When he speaks of alignment, Meyer is primarily talking about alignment to behavioral norms that he has established for the team. His approach to results begins with an approach to practice and preparation. He coaches players that every step they take on every play must be at full speed, with maximum effort. Only through this level of commitment, will the team be able to execute at the level necessary to win championships. But moreover, he knows that most individuals cannot deliver that level of effort in every practice repetition or on every play in a game, relying only on their own personal resolve. Meyer knows that it must come with a commitment to a purpose bigger than yourself. And for his organization, he emphasizes that purpose as your accountability to your teammates. Meyer preaches a philosophy of "Nine Units Strong", meaning that each position must first work as a unit at the highest possible level, and then be accountable to the other units to deliver on that level of performance to all of the other eight units. Within each position unit he creates a balance of unity and competition within that group, for all players in that position group to push each other and support each other to be the best that they can be. That creates a bond within that small group that builds a powerful sense of oneness within the group.

 Coaching Point: Since One-ness cultures tend to be more inwardly-focused, it is important for the organization to hold itself and each other accountable. Leaders should focus on ensuring that they are driving continuous gains in productivity.

But the oneness extends beyond that group as well. "Nine Units Strong" speaks to the responsibility that each group feels towards the other that they must perform well to not let the other units down – that success can only come when all nine units are performing up to their potential. But it also infers that no one unit is more important than another, and that each part of the broader team may need to take a leading or supporting role from time to time, or to outperform at times when another unit is lagging, as needed in certain circumstances.

Team First

These are classic characteristics of the cultural archetype that I call a One-ness culture. In general, a One-ness culture type prioritizes a focus on the team before the individual, the organization over any one particular function. It is a people-first approach that gets its strength from within. It is often manifested in a matrixed organization, where all functions and business units are interdependent. Organizations that emphasize alignment will often refer to the word "culture" the most, communicating that their team-oriented environment is the source of their competitive advantage.

Ford Motor Company, under the leadership of Alan Mulally beginning in 2006 is a good example of a One-ness culture. Prior to 2006, the culture at Ford was siloed and competitive. Meetings were battlegrounds for executives focused on hoarding resources and ensuring self-preservation[32]. Under Mulally, the separate global units were combined, to both encourage idea sharing and innovation, but more importantly to focus each of the units on the overall goal of the corporation, "one Ford", winning. He placed a premium on transparent communication and collaborative decision-making across the units and severely discouraged any moves by executives that were seen as maximizing units over the whole.

 Coaching Point: At their worst, One-ness cultures can become bureaucratic, so instilling effective processes and support for decision-making is critical.

The cultural transformation led to a massively successful business transformation. When Mulally took over in 2006, Ford had just turned in its worst performance in its history, a $12.7B loss, and its debt was at junk status. It was widely accepted that Ford would file for bankruptcy[33]. But upon his retirement in 2014, Ford celebrated its 19th consecutive profitable quarter[34]. Mulally often credits the "One Ford" movement as the driver for the historical turnaround.

A focus on "one-ness" is often employed in turnaround environments. When organizations are under-performing, improving results will require change from all parts of the organization which is always

[32](Hoffman, 2012)
[33](Kraemer, 2015)
[34](Gallo, 2014)

difficult. Moreover, it will require individuals to sometimes sacrifice their short term goals in deference to the larger organization's needs.

 Coaching Point: A One-ness culture requires individual sacrifice and will benefit from a more supportive leadership approach.

Sometimes an emphasis on alignment can be taken too far as well. At its extreme, it can create an "Us Against the World" environment. This was an approach used by Steve Jobs during his first run at Apple, especially during the development of the Macintosh. While it can create unbelievably strong internal bonds, it can grow to the point of alienating anyone outside the group and turn a great vision into a bloody jihad.

Aside from those extremes, a focus on alignment has certainly been successful for many types of organizations. It tends to be a great fit for organizations that are primarily talent dependent, as they encourage people to help one another. It also fits well into industries where markets are relatively stable. Since alignment-focused cultures tend to be more inwardly-focused, it can have difficulty continuously adapting to quickly shifting market environments. Conversely, they tend to thrive when the organization has a strong sense of purpose, or some higher calling that it serves.

 Coaching Point: One-ness culture tend to be inwardly focused, so they will be more effective in more mature markets. In rapidly changing markets, they can struggle.

Successful leaders focused on alignment must be effective delegators. Urban Meyer gave his position coaches tremendous autonomy to run their units, as you might imagine with a mantra like "Nine Units Strong". But that requires that the leader do a great job of providing clarity of vision and well-defined expectations, to ensure that all leaders can align to them. As such, they have a bias towards coaching and empowering others.

Coaching Point: One way of creating the "one-ness" environment is by enabling the entire team to participate fully through proactive delegation. Without it, it feels more like "your team" instead of "our team"

CHARACTERISTICS OF THE ONE-NESS CULTURE	
Leadership Attributes	**Business Attributes**
Leadership Style – Delegating	Common Markets – Mature
Common Disc Profile – Supportive	Key Metric – Employee Engagement
Managerial Focus – Productivity	Innovation Focus – Breakthrough
Key Skill – Decision-Making	Productivity
Example Leader – Urban Meyer	Striving for – Purpose
	Fascinated by – Alignment

FIGURE 16. CHARACTERISTICS OF THE ONE-NESS CULTURE

■ EXECUTION

When Bill Walsh joined the San Francisco 49ers in 1979, he was shocked. Raised under the legendary taskmaster, Paul Brown, Walsh could not believe the lack of operational discipline across all aspects of the organization. From the football field to the front office, all he saw was chaos[35]. The 49ers went 2-14 in 1978, and based on what he found, he was surprised they won that many. If the DeBartolo family (the owners of the 49ers at the time) wanted a more fundamentally sound organization, they brought in the right man.

As we have discussed previously, Walsh was an execution-oriented leader, and that orientation was a key to the culture that he built in San Francisco. Where Meyer might focus on the team first, for Walsh, it was always on his Standard of Performance. The Standard of Performance defined in great detail what Walsh believed was an acceptable level of performance. He established standards for every position – for players on the field, and even for front office personnel.

. . . .

[35](Walsh B. , 2009)

He created those standards with no regard for what level of capability currently resided in each role. The Standard was the Standard, and everyone would be measured against the Standard – not against last year's performance, and not against whomever played that position before.

 Coaching Point: Execution cultures place a big focus on key performance indicators. Create clarity around the metrics that matter, and measure people and the business against them publicly and often.

He loved his players, but ultimately, players come and go – they were just a means to an end. Walsh had a vision in his head of what flawless execution looked like on the playing field, and he was constantly in pursuit of that vision. And to that end, he would exchange out any player in favor of one that he thought could deliver better performance. After all, he benched, and eventually traded, arguably the best quarterback ever to play the game – Joe Montana – because he felt that at the time, Steve Young, might have been able to perform better.

But Walsh's vision didn't stop at the football field. He carefully planned, and drove the relentless execution of every aspect of operations of the San Francisco 49ers. He even wrote the scripts for how the receptionists should answer the phone. Nothing was left to chance. Walsh would plan, down to the minute, every practice and every meeting for the entire football season – before the season ever started. Every callisthenic, every drill, every film study, every day, of every week, for the entire season[36].

From his perspective, it was the coach's responsibility to enable the highest level of productivity out of every player, and complete organization of every aspect of preparation paved the way for that. As a result, the player's only responsibility was to execute. And flawless

. . . .
[36](Walsh & Billick, Finding the Winning Edge, 1997)

execution of his vision, his Standard of Performance, would be the winning edge that his team would need to win championships.

 Coaching Point: Delivering to the plan is paramount in an Execution culture. And that focus trumps loyalty to people, which can seem harsh at times.

And Walsh believed that culture precedes results. He once said, "Winners start acting like winners before they start winning". He believed that the leader should expect professional attention to all controllable details, and it will spill over into all aspects of the organization's performance. To Walsh, culture is the "behavioral infrastructure"[37] of the organization. So, despite his popular reputation as a "mad scientist", at his core, Walsh had a maniacal focus on execution, and the process and behavioral discipline that made it possible. These are classic attributes of an execution-focused culture, and Walsh rode that culture to three Super Bowl titles.

Metrics, Metrics, Metrics

Execution-focused cultures have many consistent and visible attributes. Firstly, they have a strong results and data orientation, usually supported with a focus on metrics. Metrics for growth, metrics for quality, metrics to measure other metrics. Not surprisingly, Microsoft is a great example of this. In his book, "The Road Ahead", written back in 1995[38], Bill Gates wrote of the discipline Microsoft applied to its marketing function. To rationalize any investment, the team would need to painstakingly analyze sales data and the elasticity of any marketing investments. Gates spoke of his new product, Microsoft Access, and its ability to gather and represent data in powerful ways. Microsoft "drank its own Kool-Aid" and built dashboards for everything – studying data to ensure that they were allocating resources

[37](Walsh B. , The Score Takes Care of Itself: My Philosophy of Leadership, 2009)
[38](Gates, 1995)

towards business outcomes in the most efficient way. That commitment continues to this day. Execution cultures are rigorous. They are constantly studying performance indicators to help the team focus on improving controllable details.

 Coaching Point: Leaders in Execution cultures must have strong aptitude and affinity for data, as it is a central rationale for making decisions and solving problems.

Process Reliability

Manufacturing organizations are notorious for manifesting execution-oriented cultures. The concepts of LEAN, Six-Sigma, and other process improvement methodologies are employed by companies focused more inwardly. The key to their success in the marketplace often depends upon them managing controllable elements like product quality, manufacturing yield and system reliability. As such they demonstrate a commitment to process reliability, which is central to an execution-focused culture.

McDonald's is an excellent example of a process-driven organization that relies on its execution culture for its competitive advantage. People are empowered, but it is freedom within a framework. In these environments, innovation tends to be focused on how to continue to improve existing processes, rather than market disrupting initiatives. Recognition is often deployed to individuals and teams that consistently meet, rather than aberrant wins that are not likely repeatable. McDonald's would rather have a very good product served up consistently, every time without fail, than an excellent product that was delivered most of the time.

 Coaching Point: Detail-orientation is a key attribute for Execution culture leaders. The willingness and the ability to elements that might seem like minutia to someone else is an ingredient for success.

Relentless in pursuing and meeting goals

Execution cultures are also relentless in pursuit of goals. We have already shared the example of Amazon's commitment to its customer service goals. But no matter how lofty, Execution cultures do not subscribe to fantasy – they want high-integrity goals. They would rather have a stretch goal that is attainable, than a wild vision that is exciting, but likely not reachable. Execution cultures prefer this, because they are highly dependent upon the accountability of leaders reaching their goals. If your competitive advantage is built on your low margin of error, then any error throughout the value chain has the power to take you down. Amazon places a high premium on consistently meeting goals, and comprehensively studies scenarios when their execution breaks down.

 Coaching Point: Execution cultures are often characterized by a pursuit of perfection. While they may never reach that destination, the pursuit ensures a level of excellence required to win in the marketplace.

At its best, an execution-oriented culture can create an environment that supports unparalleled business performance. But it has a dark side as well. When taken too far, the pressure to perform can take its toll on employees. Amazon has developed a reputation as a very difficult place to work. A common internal joke at Amazon is that is a place "where over-achievers go to feel bad about themselves". Their rate of burnout of employees has been reported often. It took its toll on Walsh too. Despite his unprecedented run of success in the 80's, Walsh pondered retirement at his apex; finding it difficult to enjoy the wins, and becoming paralyzed by the thought of losing even one game.

An emphasis on execution is indicated for markets that are more mature. It is difficult to build in repeatable standards if the environment is unstable. As mentioned, organizations with a heavy element of manufacturing or production thrive in an execution-focused culture. Also, industries with higher-risk working conditions like Oil & Gas, or Construction often stress an execution mindset.

These mature markets and risk-heavy industries often present high-impact decisions and/or decisions with a long duration of impact. As such, leaders that are successful in these environments tend to have a cautious personality[39] that does not make sudden moves, and never without strong data support. To be successful, they must be patient teachers, as many people around them may not have the passion for perfection, or the perseverance to get there.

 Coaching Point: Execution cultures are best aligned to mature markets, and especially to high-risk environments. As such, cautious, calm and more methodical leaders tend to be the best fit.

CHARACTERISTICS OF THE EXECUTION CULTURE	
Leadership Attributes	**Business Attributes**
Leadership Style - Detail-oriented Common Disc Profile – Cautious Managerial Focus - Delivering on Plan Key Skill - Problem-solving Example Leader - Bill Walsh	Common Markets - Mature Key Metric – Operational KPIs Innovation Focus – Breakthrough Process Improvement Striving for - Perfection Fascinated by - Data

FIGURE 17. CHARACTERISTICS OF THE EXECUTION CULTURE

■ CUSTOMER/MARKET-DRIVEN

Unlike Walsh, who invented and adhered to, his "West Coast Offense", Bill Belichick never met a system he didn't like. He was a keen student of many systems over the years, working under several great football minds, and learning from all of them. He spent much of his

. . . .
[39](Harris, n.d.)

time on the defensive side of football, and as such, has spent most of his career dissecting the other team's offensive approach, and devising a way to beat it. So, as we discussed in the strategy section, his success has been characterized by his obsession of studying the opponent, and adapting his approach to exploit their weakness. He has been characterized as a genius in his ability to master so many different philosophies, and to adopt the best approach to get the job done, even from week to week.

But his success has not been built on the skillsets of a cadre of highly skilled players, like that of Chuck Noll and the Pittsburgh Steelers of the 1970's. Those Pittsburgh teams were highly successful, but that success can be attributed to a large nucleus of Hall of Fame players that were acquired at roughly the same time, and the fact that they stayed together for their entire career. As that nucleus retired, the Steelers dynasty came to an end. The Patriots since 2001, have been the most successful franchise in NFL history, winning five Super Bowl titles. And they have done so with only one player that has been on all of those teams. Moreover, the Patriots have often won championships without superior talent, confounding the experts and opposing coaches. So Belichick has proven he can win without superior talent within the team, but with a relentless focus on what is going on outside the team.

These are the hallmark characteristics of a customer or market-driven culture. The focus is on the customer, the market, and/or the competition, and they align their resources strategically to win. They foster a competitive environment where winning is everything, and where the prize for winning is in clear sight to all. More so than other cultures, they talk about market share, instead of just growth. They do so because Customer-driven cultures tend to thrive in companies that participate in highly competitive markets. And so, to win, they must take customers and market share from their competitors. To do so, they spend significant resources on market and competitive analysis.

For those of you that follow pro football, Belichick has a reputation for aggressively pursuing market research.

 Coaching Point: Customer/Market-driven cultures are obsessed with the customer. Successful companies focus on pursuing and creating unique insights that enable them to take share from competitors

This is War

Companies like PepsiCo are good examples of this. Pepsi executives wake up every morning thinking about how they are going to be beat Coca-Cola. I have a personal anecdote that can help draw a picture of the culture there. My first job out of college was with PepsiCo, where I was responsible for a cluster of grocery store accounts. Not long after I took the job, I was given a challenge. The President of PepsiCo was coming to my city, and was going to tour a couple of my stores. My boss informed me that I was to have these stores in amazing shape, and all representing Pepsi well. Among several initiatives, I had a team of merchandisers come through the stores to clean and straighten every Pepsi can and bottle on every aisle in the stores. When the President arrived, the stores looked amazing, and I walked him down the aisle of one store, sharing with him our sales tactics and results in this particular chain. But as I was doing so, I noted that as he was walking past the Coca-Cola products, he was dragging his hand across the product on the shelf, messing up their facing and straightness on the shelf – the President of the company! I don't think he even consciously knew he was doing it. That was the "cola wars", and that is the culture that war creates – a fiercely competitive environment that will do anything to win.

 Coaching Point: Customer/Market cultures are obsessed with winning. As such, successful leaders tend to be aggressive, results-oriented, with a more dominant personality. This culture is not a place for the quiet or timid.

Customer or market-driven cultures are often more focused on the customers and markets that they serve, than they are in the products and services they offer. They invest resources in surveys and any other tools for discovering and exploiting unmet customer or market needs. Enterprise Rent-A-Car is an example of this type of company. Enterprise competes in a seemingly commoditized market that is highly competitive, and ostensibly, very price elastic. Moreover, success is highly correlated to the amount of advertising and promotion you do, and the amount you pay for favorable positions at airport pickup locations. Enterprise invests much less than the majors in advertising, and often does not even invest in airport slots at all. They developed an innovative approach based on the insight they received from their customers that they often need to get a ride to the rental car facility. But even within their niche, they have a staunch commitment to customer surveys. They pursue and analyze more customer survey data than any other rental car company. And it pays off. Enterprise is the largest and fastest growing rental car company in the U.S., and their customer loyalty is tops in the market[40]. Their competitive advantage is their near fascination with listening to, and understanding, their customer better than their competitors.

 Coaching Point: Leaders in the Customer/Market-driven culture must be able to demonstrate, and authentically possess, a complete fascination and passion for their customers. For the organization to develop the customer intimacy required for success, they must be able to impart that passion to the rest of the organization.

Do Your Job

People are important in the Customer/Market Culture, but they value people with direct customer experience and with unique market insights. In an extreme view, they tend to look at people simply as

. . . .
[40](News, 2015)

tools that can help them win. As such, they tend to recruit for specific skills and capabilities, and create clear operating plans for them to help them execute. The most common representation of Bill Belichick's organizational culture is "Do Your Job". Belichick clearly understands the jobs that need to be done in order to win, and recruits for them. By often refusing to sign big-name players to massive contracts, he has made a name for himself by finding value in less than marquee players that can fulfill a specific role on his football team.

When taken to the extreme, a customer or market-oriented culture can seem a bit heartless to employees. Critics might say that players are somewhat fungible to Belichick – that if he can find a player that can do that job for less money, he will replace them immediately. The loyalty is to results, not the people. That may sound heartless, but when led effectively, Customer/Market Cultures can be very transparent internally – sharing this value very clearly and openly. If so, the culture can be lauded as honest, as opposed to heartless.

A great example in the corporate world is Netflix. Netflix was an early disrupter to the video rental business, but is now in a very competitive space with well-funded competitors. As such, they would need great performance from their people if they are going to be successful in such a competitive, and highly technical space. Moreover, their space is in constant flux, and they need people that understand their role, and can operate independently. From the very beginning, they espoused a culture of "freedom and responsibility", where people were empowered to think and create independently, but also fully responsible for generating outstanding results. Hard work is nice, but from their perspective, irrelevant. If you could generate fantastic results in half the time, fine, take the rest of the week off. They value providing context, instead of instituting overbearing control. And in return, they invest in people development, and pay at the top of the market. But above all else, they expect high performance. They shocked a lot of people when they publicly stated that in their culture, "'A' players get a paycheck, and everyone else gets a generous severance package[41]".

 Coaching Point: The Customer/Market culture prioritizes goals and delivering on high expectations defined by customers. Leaders must be comfortable managing performance based on objective results – sometimes results that are not fully in their control. The outcome is the outcome, the customer defines it, and that is the standard that we are measured by, and held accountable to.

Bill Belichick runs an organization in a highly competitive marketplace, and has been successful by creating a culture where people are expected to "do your job", and to do it very well, or the organization will find someone who can. At the same time, players want to play for the New England Patriots and Bill Belichick, and many players speak very well of the organization after they leave it. Evidently, a winning culture can attract winning players, and when done transparently, a culture that demands high performance, or else, can be seen as fair and honest.

Customer or market-driven cultures tend to be successful in growing markets, especially in highly competitive spaces. It supports the effort of getting all of the resources of the organization focused on the customer, and winning.

Leaders that are successful in this type of culture are results-oriented. Their focus is mostly on the task, and their personality is often described as more dominant. They may not be the warmest people, but they tend to get the job done. Belichick's demeanor at press conferences is legendary, and gives insight into his stoic personality. They do not shy away from difficult conversations, and they often embrace conflict as part of whatever 'war' they are engaged in, whether it is based on cola or something else.

[41](Mccord, 2014)

Coaching Point: Customer/Market cultures are best-suited to high-growth stage markets where winning today will have significant implications for success for years to come. Leaders are often characterized as "no-nonsense", results-oriented leaders.

CHARACTERISTICS OF THE CUSTOMER/MARKET CENTRIC CULTURE	
Leadership Attributes	**Business Attributes**
Leadership Style – Driving, Aggressive	Common Markets – Growth
Common Disc Profile – Dominant	Key Metric – Market Share
Managerial Focus – Beating Forecast	Innovation Focus – Customer Insights
Key Skill – Customer/Market Intimacy	Striving for – Growth
Example Leader – Bill Belichick	Fascinated by – The Customer

**FIGURE 18. CHARACTERISTICS OF
THE CUSTOMER/MARKET CENTRIC CULTURE**

■ COLLABORATION

Mack Brown took over as head coach of the Texas Longhorns on Thursday, December 4, 1997[42]. The offer was extended and accepted over a dinner that concluded just before midnight. Coach Brown was scheduled to appear at the official press conference on the afternoon of the next day. But before then, he managed to spend the morning speaking with former coach Darrell Royal. And in the car to the press conference, he made two phone calls; one to Eddie Joseph of the Texas High School Coaches Association, and one to Joe Jamail, a prominent Houston attorney, and a large benefactor to the athletic program of the University. Brown had not yet been in his role for 12hrs, but he had proactively reached out to a beloved former Longhorn coach who was the key to winning back the fan base, an influential high school coaching administrator who would be instrumental in building relationships with the people who could connect him with the talent he would need to win, and to the biggest of the BMDs (big money donors), who could donate the funds he would need to ensure that

[42](Brown M. , One Heartbeat, 2001)

he had the facilities he needed to win at the highest level. Within 12 hours, he had successfully invested in relationships with his base of customers, his cradle of talent, and his source of funding. Is he a master of culture, or simply a natural networker?

Mack Brown was certainly an excellent coach, recruiter, and role model for young players. But his ability to connect to multiple stakeholders, and encourage them to work together towards a common goal, may have been his biggest source of competitive advantage. And he was wildly successful in reaching that goal. Over the next 12 years, no team would win more games than the Texas Longhorns. And, success of that duration in college football is rare, where talent turns over every 3 years or so. Sustained success like Brown's came from an effective culture; and in this case, a collaboration-oriented culture.

 Coaching Point: Leaders in a Collaboration culture must be inclusive, building relationships and proactively managing the stakeholders that will provide the access to the resources that they will need to win.

Pursuing the Big Win

Organizations with a Collaboration culture spend a lot of their attention looking outside the firm, connecting to stakeholders, just like Mack Brown did. Their strength lies in people, but not just their own employees. They connect with customers, partners, supporters, and excel at making allies wherever they go. Unlike an execution-focused culture, they look outside of their own core process or resources to help them reach their goals.

This is important, because Collaboration cultures are often associated with organizations that are trying to reach the top of the mountain. Instead of manageable goals that are within their sphere of control, they tend to embrace larger goals that they could never deliver on alone. And unlike the Customer/Market Culture, they value relationships highly; for more than just the revenue they can provide at the moment. They tend to be chosen by organizations that are focused on the horizon, in pursuit of some larger vision, and encouraging others to come along for the ride with them.

Uber and Lyft are good examples of the collaboration-centric culture. Their business model is built on their ability to influence several different stakeholder groups to collaborate towards a common goal. They must build a brand that consumers trust, that changes their perceptions of ride-sharing, and that disrupts the long held notion of the taxi cab. Concurrently, they must assemble a group of drivers who act as the supply to this exchange, or there would be no cars waiting to pick you up. But aside from the customers and the labor, there are other stakeholders whom both companies must win over to ensure their sustainability. These groups include lawmakers who they must convince to reshape legislation to allow their disruptive model to exist, the lobbyists who sadly control most our lawmakers, and the general public, whose perception can sway quickly. On the surface, they make a technology platform that connects riders to drivers. But to be successful, they depend upon a collaborative culture that brings together a broad set of stakeholders to redefine public transportation.

And like many collaborative companies, they tend to take on audacious goals. Lyft has partnered with General Motors to create and finance cars for potential drivers to remove impediments to growing their base of supply. Uber has been extremely proactive in the area of driverless cars, seeking to perhaps one day remove a key cost from the system and completely reinvent auto travel.

 Coaching Point: A Collaboration culture is well-suited to organizations that are seeking new ground, or truly disruptive business models that will require support from a wide array of stakeholders.

The collaboration-oriented culture is one commonly effective for new entrants to a market, or to emerging markets, where companies often don't have the resources to deliver the entire value chain. So, they must have a culture that facilitates partnering with external stakeholders for additional pieces of the value chain or even financing. As such, communication, influence and relationship-building skills are highly valued within the firm.

Many technology companies tend to have a heavy focus on external collaboration as they are reliant on partner networks to fulfill the entire solution for customers. Companies like Apple and Salesforce.com depend upon networks of developers and partners that turn their technology into the final solution that creates value for their users, and collaborating effectively is critical to their success.

 Coaching Point: To be successful in a Collaboration culture, leaders must demonstrate an ability to inspire and influence external organizations to join them in their effort. These skills and this culture are especially relevant in startups and early-stage companies that must partner to be successful.

Collaboration-focused companies require leaders that are more externally-focused, and that build relationships easily. They must have a broad understanding of the industry over and above their unique aspect of it. You generally see leaders with a more extroverted personality. They enthusiastically share their vision, and inspire others to join them on the journey.

CHARACTERISTICS OF THE COLLABORATION CULTURE	
Leadership Attributes	**Business Attributes**
Leadership Style – Inclusive	Common Markets – Early Stage
Common Disc Profile – Inspiring	Key Metric – Revenue Growth
Managerial Focus – Stakeholder Management	Innovation Focus – Disruptive Business Models
Key Skill – Influence	Striving for – New Ground
Example Leader – Mack Brown	Fascinated by – Relationships

FIGURE 19. CHARACTERISTICS OF THE COLLABORATION CULTURE

These archetypes explore and explain four unique organizational cultures. Standing back from the four, we see that they define cultures according to two primary axes; a dominant focus either internal or external to the organization, and a dominant focus towards either people or goals/tasks. Organizing them into a 2x2 matrix, they become a complete organizational culture framework.

	Internal	External
Goal/Task	**Execution** *Leadership Attributes* Leadership Style – Detail-oriented Common Disc Profile – Cautious Managerial Focus – Delivering on Plan Key Skill – Problem-solving Example Leader – Bill Walsh *Business Attributes* Market Stage – Mature Key Metric – Operational KPIs Innovation Focus – Breakthrough Process Improvement Striving for – Perfection Fascinated by – Data	**Customer/Market Centric** *Leadership Attributes* Leadership Style – Driving, Aggressive Common Disc Profile – Dominant Managerial Focus – Beating Forecast Key Skill – Customer/Market Intimacy Example Leader – Bill Belichick *Business Attributes* Market Stage – Growth Key Metric – Market Share Innovation Focus – Customer Insights Striving for – Growth Fascinated by – The Customer
People	**One-ness** *Leadership Attributes* Leadership Style – Delegating Common Disc Profile – Supportive Managerial Focus – Productivity Key Skill – Decision-Making Example Leader – Urban Meyer *Business Attributes* Market Stage – Mature Key Metric – Employee Engagement Innovation Focus – Breakthrough Productivity Striving for – Purpose Fascinated by – Alignment	**Collaboration** *Leadership Attributes* Leadership Style – Inclusive Common Disc Profile – Inspiring Managerial Focus – Stakeholder Management Key Skill – Influence Example Leader – Mack Brown *Business Attributes* Market Stage – Early Stage Key Metric – Revenue Growth Innovation Focus – Disruptive Business Models Striving for – New Ground Fascinated by – Relationships

FIGURE 20. THE FOUR ORGANIZATIONAL CULTURE ARCHETYPES

Determining your Unique Culture Recipe

These cultural archetypes are useful in explaining organizational culture, but of course, rarely is a company's culture fully explained by just one. Every organization combines a blend of these attributes to create a culture that is uniquely theirs and hopefully suited to the environment they are operating in, the goals they are pursuing, and the person charged with leading it.

That does not necessarily mean that you can simply pick and choose the elements you like from any quadrant. A great culture must contain attributes, like the leadership and business characteristics listed above, that are mutually reinforcing. As an example, a Detail-oriented leader may be ineffective, or may frustrate others, if they were put in charge of an early stage growth company. The cultural environment within a startup environment would not be conducive to a detail-oriented, leader, or a process improvement managerial focus – one would end up stifling or cancelling out the other.

The characteristics listed in each quadrant are generally mutually-reinforcing, creating the opportunity for an organizational culture with a virtuous cycle, where each element feeds the other. When you are designing your culture, you should proactively look for supporting and contradicting elements to ensure you are designing a culture that is fundamentally sound.

But an organizational culture does not exist in a vacuum from other elements of the business. A great culture is the one that:

- supports your vision and purpose
- is consistent with the results you are pursuing
- reinforces your strategy
- matches your leadership style.

Great businesses design great cultures that fit them, and reinforce what they trying to accomplish. Hewlett Packard is one of the original Silicon Valley success stories, and its prolonged period of success must be attributed, at least to a degree to the culture established by the founders. They created and broadly communicated their blueprint for the culture of the organization in the "HP Way"[43]. The HP Way was their manifesto on What, How, and Why" of Hewlett Packard, and communicated the key tradeoffs it was making in its culture.

The HP Way

1. Profit. To recognize that profit is the best single measure of our contribution to society and the ultimate source of our corporate strength. We should attempt to achieve the maximum possible profit consistent with our other objectives.

2. Customers. To strive for continual improvement in the quality, usefulness, and value of the products and services we offer our customers.

3. Field of Interest. To concentrate our efforts, continually seeking new opportunities for growth but limiting our involvement to fields in which we have capability and can make a contribution.

4. Growth. To emphasize growth as a measure of strength and a requirement for survival.

5. Employees. To provide employment opportunities for HP people that include the opportunity to share in the company's success, which they help make possible. To provide for them job security based on performance, and to provide the opportunity for personal satisfaction that comes from a sense of accomplishment in their work.

6. Organization. To maintain an organizational environment that fosters individual motivation, initiative and creativity, and a wide latitude of freedom in working toward established objectives and goals.

7. Citizenship. To meet the obligations of good citizenship by making contributions to the community and to the institutions in our society which generate the environment in which we operate.

FIGURE 21. THE HP WAY

. . . .

[43](Packard, 2006)

When you break down the HP Way, it called out and communicated expectations on several key cultural aspects:

Vision or Purpose. Profit is the reason we are in business, and clarified that there was no mixed purpose. Our purpose for being is to make a profit. We want to help the planet, and to do "social good", but our method of doing so is by making profits, and then apportioning some of them to the communities we support. So, our leaders' focus should be on producing a profit, not on doing social good. That may sound heartless, but Hewlett and Packard were anything but heartless. They were also not vain. They knew that the best way they could contribute to the world was through their technology, and by contributing money generated by profits, not by symbolic gestures that are often more about self-fulfillment, instead of truly helping their fellow man.

Results Measurement. As a technology company, they understood that they understood that they were in a growing industry, so the benchmark for success was going to have to reflect that. So, in their case, revenue and market share would be the way that they kept score, which then defines that they would allocate a disproportionate percentage of their resources to their go-to-market organization. That strategy was supported by an industry-leading sales team that received a consistently above-average investment in sales training, tools and resources.

Strategy. The HP Way stated clearly that they will create value for customers with the products and services they create, and that they will be known for quality. They didn't say they wanted to be cutting edge – they want to create useful products for their customer segment, and to deliver those products with a high expectation of quality. While their products were going to be important, they did not call them out specifically. Instead, they referred more to a market segment that they were going to serve. It also defined their innovation strategy. They would not be a

Google, which values unstructured exploration for the potential it represents. Any innovation project would have to be initiated by a clearly articulated market need that it was created to resolve.

Leadership & Relationship to Employees. The HP Way called out that employees would be given freedom to pursue their passions to a degree, but that that freedom will be directed at specific goals that the company will establish. So, it stressed alignment, but not too itself, or to an ideal, but to a set of goals around growing the business, and the profits generated by that growth.

So, you can see that HP consciously chose an organizational culture that closely aligns to the Customer/Market Centric Culture archetype. They did so because it was consistent with the goals they had for the company, the external market environment that they were operating in, the strategy they were pursuing, and how Hewlett and Packard saw themselves as leaders and the relationship they felt the organization should have with employees.

 Coaching Point: As you craft your desired culture, keep in mind that it should be consistent with the goals you have for the organization, the market environment where you play, the strategy you pursue, and your natural leadership style.

The HP Way is both comprehensive, yet simple, and it has provided clarity around the organizational culture at HP for nearly 80 years. The careful design of their organizational culture has sustained the company through the often brutal cyclicality of the technology industry, and allowed it to create great products for customers, exciting jobs for millions of employees, and significant wealth for shareholders.

CHALK TALK:

Consider the attributes of the four culture archetypes shared in Figure X.

- Which elements are most aligned to your organizational purpose or vision?

- Which archetype matches up best to your market environment?

- Which archetype aligns best to the strategy that you have chosen for the organization?

- What type of leadership style is going to be the most effective, and how does your own leadership style fit into this matrix?

	Internal	External
Goal/Task	**Execution** *Leadership Attributes* Leadership Style – Detail-oriented Common Disc Profile – Cautious Managerial Focus – Delivering on Plan Key Skill – Problem-solving Example Leader – Bill Walsh *Business Attributes* Market Stage – Mature Key Metric – Operational KPIs Innovation Focus – Breakthrough Process Improvement Striving for – Perfection Fascinated by – Data	**Customer/Market Centric** *Leadership Attributes* Leadership Style – Driving, Aggressive Common Disc Profile – Dominant Managerial Focus - Beating Forecast Key Skill – Customer/Market Intimacy Example Leader – Bill Belichick *Business Attributes* Market Stage – Growth Key Metric – Market Share Innovation Focus – Customer Insights Striving for – Growth Fascinated by – The Customer
People	**One-ness** *Leadership Attributes* Leadership Style – Delegating Common Disc Profile – Supportive Managerial Focus – Productivity Key Skill – Decision-Making Example Leader – Urban Meyer *Business Attributes* Market Stage – Mature Key Metric – Employee Engagement Innovation Focus – Breakthrough Productivity Striving for – Purpose Fascinated by – Alignment	**Collaboration** *Leadership Attributes* Leadership Style – Inclusive Common Disc Profile – Inspiring Managerial Focus – Stakeholder Management Key Skill – Influence Example Leader - Mack Brown *Business Attributes* Market Stage – Early Stage Key Metric – Revenue Growth Innovation Focus – Disruptive Business Models Striving for – New Ground Fascinated by – Relationships

FIGURE 22. THE FOUR ORGANIZATIONAL ARCHETYPES

DEFINING YOUR CULTURE

We began our discussion on organizational culture by exploring some of Urban Meyer's philosophies, and how they have been central to his success. Meyer sees a simple, causal relationship from culture to results, and that it all begins with the leader – Leaders create culture > Culture drives behavior > Behavior produces results. So, the leader is responsible for the culture of the organization, and to define the behaviors that are consistent with producing results.

In his book, titled "Above the Line", he describes his belief in the concept of alignment – having everyone demonstrating behaviors that are aligned with the goals of the organization. Meyer realized that to get true alignment, he must have simplicity – to make it clear what behaviors are aligned with success, and which are not. He uses the terms "above the line" and "below the line", to describe which ones are consistent with, and in opposition to, the culture of the team, respectively. While many of us may describe organizational culture in shades of grey, architects of highly effective culture do their best to describe them in black and white. When successful you create the "behavioral infrastructure", as Bill Walsh described it, which will form the foundation and strength of your organizational culture.

We are Family

Let's revisit the example of Mack Brown, and his Texas Longhorns, and his vision for "Winning Championships with Good Kids Who Graduate". We described his culture as Collaborative, and his success at building relationships with, and bringing together, a broad set of stakeholders, to support the goals of the organization. Brown clearly demonstrated support for the proverb, "It takes a village to support a child". That quote is fitting, giving the acknowledgement that his players are "Kids", or specifically, 18-21 year olds. And most of those young men, who would be so central to his success, would be leaving their families for the first time in their lives, to come and play football for him.

Coach Brown knew, that for him to be successful in encouraging parents to send him their kids, and to ensure those kids would be successful at the University of Texas, it would take a "village". It would take a family. But claiming you have a family atmosphere is easy to do. To make it real, you have to bring that culture to life in visible terms in ways that his recruits/players, and their families, could see and feel.

During the recruiting process, he spent an inordinate amount of time learning about a recruit's family. Coach Brown clearly took responsibility for "the kids", telling parents that he would take care of them, when they were with him at the University of Texas. When he spoke of the leadership of the program, it was always "Sally (his wife) and I", never just him, just like there was a Mom and Dad there. Players often came to their house for dinners, and Sally always knew the players and even their girlfriends if they had one. Recruits and incoming freshmen were assigned a "Big Brother", whose job it was to ensure that the newcomer assimilated successfully, and was thriving in the program. Seniors were afforded special leadership roles within the team, allowing them to self-police and set the tone for the younger players just like family elders. Mack had established a culture of the organization focused on "family values" that supported his vision of "Winning championships with good kids that graduate".

 Coaching Point: If you can't objectively "prove" your culture by observable behaviors, processes, and rituals, then you may not have the culture you think you do.

Mack demonstrated the culture he wanted to create, but he also defined cultural expectations for his extended "family" as well. He felt that the existing fan base was lackadaisical towards the team, and that they did not demonstrate an appropriate level of spirit that was consistent with winning programs. But he didn't say "y'all improve your team spirit". He described what he expected to see as observable proof of improved fan morale - tangible evidence of an improved culture in the fan base. He established a motto to communicate what he expected. "Come Early, Be Loud, Stay Late, Wear Orange." None of these elements were chosen haphazardly.

"Come Early". To be successful, his teams needed to be able to start games fast, to bring an intensity to the opposition from the first play. But football is a game that is swayed not only by talent, but by emotion, and he knew his team would feed off the energy provided by a stadium that was full at kickoff. But over the 80s and 90s, the students had begun to make a habit of showing up late in the 1st quarter; more focused on their pregame parties than on the game itself. Mack knew this behavior would create an energy "flywheel" that mutually reinforced both the fans and the players.

"Be Loud". Brown knew that loud stadiums provide a significant advantage to the home team. A rowdy home crowd can make it very difficult for opposing teams to communicate changes to plays on the field, especially on crucial downs, meaningfully tipping the odds in favor of the defense. Texas fans had become increasingly subdued; perhaps too civilized for the good of the

team. He wanted to make sure that Darrell K Royal stadium would not be an easy place to play for opponents, but would be an exciting place for fans and Longhorn players.

"Stay Late". Above all, and without reproach, Mack Brown is a gentleman. He insisted that his team always demonstrate good sportsmanship, and he wanted the fans to do the same. From his perspective, one behavior that demonstrates character is to stay until the end of the game, regardless of the score. Brown reinforced and strongly promoted the tradition that no matter the outcome of the game, that all fans, players and coaches raised their right hand in the Hook 'Em Horns handsign, and sing the school song, "The Eyes of Texas", at the end of the game. It was a clear manifestation of Brown's definition of sportsmanship, and perhaps a reflection of how we "raise kids" at the University of Texas. And it is a very visible manifestation of respect that players and fans have for each other, and for The University.

"Wear Orange". For years, students at The University prided themselves in their appearance on gameday. Each year they sought out new ways to create an outfit for game days that signified their support of the team, but without signaling it too obviously. To Brown, fans spent more effort trying to look cool, instead of looking like a Texas Longhorn fan. He let people know it was OK, and actually expected, to wear burnt orange at the games. It was a simple, and very visible way for fans to demonstrate their alignment to the culture that Mack had set for the organization. Almost overnight, the look of the stadium changed demonstratively, again a very visible signal that the culture around The University of Texas football program had changed.

That cultural transformation translated to business results. When Brown arrived in 1998, season ticket purchases were at a low point, at just over 38,000. But by 2010, they had increased to over 84,000, and the athletic program revenue had more than quadrupled. His ability to create a family encouraged fans to buy more tickets and merchandise, and donors to contribute more funds. And those funds financed significant improvement in facilities that attracted better players. He had created the flywheel effect that effective cultures foster.

 Coaching Point: Don't leave culture up to chance. Specifically define the behavior you expect from your internal and external stakeholders

We Are a Team, Not a Family

Earlier, I shared Netflix as an example of a Customer/Market-Driven culture. But their culture was not determined by some 2x2 chart, or even by the Harvard Business Review article describing their unique culture[44]. It is defined by the behaviors that are called out and supported by management, and the way those behaviors are recognized and rewarded. Patty McCord was the head of HR for Netflix, and released a slide deck that summed up their corporate culture. It contained some powerful statements and bold expectations for company leaders, the behaviors desired of them. But most of all, it included a description of their nine values, and example behavior standards for each one. They were all described using action verbs to ensure that they were painting a picture of observable behaviors – making them as tangible as possible.

As an example, and fitting for their role as an innovative company in an emerging technology space, they named Courage as a core value. But as a company that is striving for a high performance culture, they described behaviors that clearly supported questioning leadership di-

. . . .
[44](Mccord, 2014)

rection, and to confront actions by peers that people might feel were inconsistent with the company values. It was an important counterpoint for a culture based on Freedom and Responsibility; to be able to challenge status quo, while also empowering everyone to act as guardrails to "too much freedom". But also as performance-focused company, they clearly communicate that they value Impact, and explicitly state the expectation that people "accomplish amazing amounts of important work". These carefully crafted and broadly communicated statements are the "behavioral infrastructure" that defines the Netflix culture.

 Coaching Point: Culture is not an esoteric idea. It is a set of expected norms for how stakeholders behave and interact with one another. Do not leave that up to interpretation. Clearly define what you expect.

Define What You Don't Want Also

As we mentioned, like strategy, culture is also about the behaviors that you do not want. Researchers and authors on culture, Steve Gruenert and Todd Whitaker state that the "The culture of any organization is shaped by the worst behavior the leader is willing to tolerate[45]." So, leaders who want a strong culture must communicate the behaviors they will not be tolerated as clearly as the ones they are looking for.

Charlie Strong took over after Mack Brown stepped down at Texas in 2013. The transition was set in motion after the Longhorns' on-field performance began to slip following the 2009 season. After one losing season in 2010, the first of the Mack Brown era at Texas, each of the next three years failed to show meaningful improvement on the field. At that time, there were claims that the culture at Texas had slipped, and that there was a lack of accountability for the players to do the work required to generate upper echelon level results,

[45](Whitaker & Gruenert, 2015)

and perhaps a lack of alignment to the kind of behavior consistent with "Good Kids".

Upon his arrival at Texas, Charlie Strong focused on the latter aspect. In keeping with his reputation as a discipline-driven, fundamentals-focused leader, he shared his "Core Values". Strong's Core Values identified both what is expected and what will not be tolerated; Honesty, Respect for Women, and a zero tolerance for drug use, theft of any kind, and possession of firearms. He also lays out strict expectations around the student aspect of their role as "student-athlete". Strong requires his players to attend all classes, to sit in the front row, and does not allow headphones to be worn while they are on campus. Some may read over these values and see them as parochial and perhaps, not terribly aspirational. But their power lies in their simplicity and clarity.

Interestingly, none of the core values have anything to do with football. Strong clearly views his role as more than someone charged with delivering results on the field, but also someone charged with molding and developing young men into productive adults. This is a powerful metaphor for corporate entities, as being in existence to not only create returns for shareholders, but also to have a positive impact on its employees and the communities in which they operate.

One might not expect to have difficulties with these types of guidelines when following a leader of a program that embraced "family values" and focused on "good kids who graduate". But before his first game at Texas, Strong had dismissed or suspended nine players, many of them slated to be in starting positions, from the team for violation of his core values. The message it sent to players, recruits and their families, the university and its alumni, and college football followers everywhere was simple – Strong had established a new culture at The University of Texas, and the boundaries and accountabilities were clear.

Coaching Point: Your actual culture will be defined by the behaviors that you call out, AND the ones that you tolerate. Great cultures are characterized by leaders that not only call out unacceptable behaviors, but that also have the will to remove those that demonstrate them – regardless of their production.

The impact of failing to make these boundaries is profound for football teams, but can be even costlier for large corporations. News stories about the behavior of several of Uber's leaders in 2016 and 2017 have multiplied, culminating in the ouster of several executives with the firm, and even the CEO being forced to step aside[46]. Reports have alleged a range of issues from sexual harassment, to IP infringement, berating drivers, and a lack of honesty in reporting public safety issues around its self-driving car performance[47]. These alleged behaviors have been costly, as independent groups estimate the reduction in enterprise value to be upwards of $10B[48]. If Culture Eats Strategy for Breakfast, then Bad Culture Eats Market Value for Lunch.

Empowering the Organization

Your ability to clarify a cultural standard, in clear observable behaviors, and what the accountabilities are for violating that standard, will determine the strength of your organizational culture. By simplifying the desired culture into behaviors, you help the organization understand the "Why" behind the desired culture, and empower everyone to make the right decisions at the right time, without micromanagement, enhancing the speed of execution. And by calling out what is clearly unacceptable, you turn "grey areas" into "no tolerance zones", and make accountability more transparent, and more tolerable to the entire organization.

. . . .

[46](Isaac, 2017)
[47](Carson, 2017)
[48](Balakrishnan, 2017)

CHALK TALK
DEFINING YOUR CULTURE

- Define cultural norms in simple messages and observable behaviors

- Culture is a series of tradeoffs, you can't do everything, so focus on what matters most

- Spend time clarifying what is not acceptable

- Your culture will be defined by the worst behavior you tolerate so be resolute in driving accountability

- Define culture through the lens of all stakeholders

- Create culture messaging that is visible to all stakeholders and make it prevalent and omnipresent

- Define what going the extra mile looks like, and don't be afraid to ask for it

DEPLOYING YOUR CULTURE

Leading Culture

While certainly up to interpretation, and impossible to prove with data, one might conclude that the degradation of on field results at the end of the Mack Brown era was connected to what may have been a degradation of the internal culture of the team. One could argue that it is inevitable. The 2nd Law of Thermodynamics states that the entropy (essentially, the level of disorder) of a system can only increase over time. That could apply to organizational culture. Essentially, through active leadership you can hold a culture together, but that without an active hand, it will eventually succumb to disorder. In a less scientific reference, any human relationship requires attention from the parties involved – be it a marriage, a friendship, or a business partnership – or it eventually withers away. So, as a leader of an organization, you are responsible, first and foremost, to actively tend to your organization's culture.

It would certainly be reasonable to say that the culture is everyone's job, and not the sole responsibility of the top leader. There are popular tenets in team leadership that define the role of the leader as changing over the lifecycle of that team. Respected team leadership models focus on the gradual transition of the leader's role from being center stage in running the team, to one that is more supportive, turning over more responsibility over to the team over time.

That philosophy is certainly a modern approach to business leadership, and provides employees with a higher degree of ownership in the team's direction. But going back to Urban Meyer's causal relationship of Leadership to Results (Leadership > Culture > Behaviors > Results), it is clear that leadership drives culture. And I would assert that the one element of leadership that cannot be delegated is the process of creating and sustaining the organizational culture.

Visible Leadership

Cultural leadership sometimes calls for strong moves that communicate your cultural message. Remember, your organizational culture will be a combination of the behaviors you call out, and the ones you allow. The Dallas Cowboys of the 1990's are an excellent case in point. During the early 90's, the Cowboys were led by Jimmy Johnson. While not necessarily known as a values-forward leader like Charlie Strong, he was nonetheless an uncompromising one where culture was concerned. He was clear in his expectations of team behavior.

On the last game of the 1992 season, in an essentially meaningless game where most of the starters were being rested, Jimmy Johnson gave reserve running back Curvin Richards the starting role. By and large, Richards ran well, and scored a touchdown, but he also lost two fumbles during the game. The next day, Johnson cut Richards, despite him being the only truly capable back-up to starter Emmitt Smith. Heading into the playoffs, Johnson was making a clear cultural statement, communicating the kind of performance he expected. Similarly, the following year, Johnson cut linebacker John Roper for sleeping in a film study session[49], despite solid performances through-

---

[49](Press, 1993)

out the beginning of the season. I am confident that neither of these moves were emotional outbursts, but calculated efforts by Johnson to clearly reinforce the culture he had designed and defined for the Dallas Cowboys. Those Cowboy teams under Johnson produced results, winning back-to-back Super Bowls.

There are similar examples from business leaders as well. Jack Welch wanted GE to have a culture of innovation, and as such, he needed leaders who would take smart risks. But to do that, he would need to have a culture that was not afraid of failure. But as a disciplined business leader, he also valued sound decision making, backed up by sound data and analysis. Soon after joining GE, he found an opportunity to make a statement on both cultural tenets. The project team that had been charged with developing the next generation compact fluorescent lightbulb (CFL) had just completed their project – on time and on budget. But, the market environment had changed since the project was initiated. Oil prices had dropped markedly, and thus, the price of home electricity had dropped as well. As such, the economic viability of the product had eroded meaningfully, and the decision was made to shelve the product and not take it into production. For many organizations, that would have meant a loss of status for the project team, or at least the feeling of defeat. But, Welch saw it as an example of what he wanted the GE culture to be. A company that takes smart bets. Some will pan out, and others will fail, but as long as the project was based on solid insights, and was run with discipline, it should be viewed as a success, and a tangible investment in the company's IP portfolio. So Welch threw a party, complete with a huge cake in the shape of a lightbulb, recognizing the team for their excellent performance. While that product IP sat dormant for years, CFL products are now creating meaningful value for GE. That party sent a clear message about what the culture at GE would stand for. And that culture that Welch created delivered amazing growth and returns during his tenure. During his 20-year tenure, the company's value increased 4,000%.

Coaching Point: Look for opportunities to make strong, visible moves that will clearly demonstrate your commitment to your desired culture. Actions speak louder than words.

Great Cultures, and Great Culture Leaders, Have Great Stories

These bold culture leadership moves become the way your culture is passed on and sustained within your organization, and how people outside the organization perceive your culture. They are shared as stories, the way history is shared in any culture. Stories of Jimmy Johnson's firing of Richards and Roper were certainly shared with rookies joining the organization, as a punctuation to the fact that the Cowboys organization did not tolerate a lack of focus on key execution issues or a lackadaisical approach to preparation. Welch's party to celebrate the CFL team and project became a story that had a clear moral to it, which sustained the notion that "GE is an innovative company that embraces smart failure".

Positive or negative, supportive or destructive to your culture, your organization has stories that are shared repeatedly. They may or may not even be true. But like any legend, once it has been told often enough, it simply becomes an accepted fact. So, as the leader of the culture, it is up to you to try to guide the narrative. Certainly, actions speak louder than words, as Johnson and Welch have proven. But there is not always the opportunity to deliver a bold move. So when the teachable moment arrives, having a great anecdote ready is the next best thing.

And as such, I would offer that all great cultural leaders are great storytellers. Football coaches tell you about their culture, and show you what matters to them by the stories they tell. Mack Brown had a powerful and true story to share to bring all of his key cultural pillars to life.

When he wanted to talk about courage and a will to win, he might tell players the story of Freddy Steinmark, a player from the 1960's who fought a difficult battle with cancer. He might share a story about Brett Robin, who is now a sports medicine doctor in Texas, if he wanted to punctuate his focus on academics, and the opportunity players have to excel in life after football. He could show what it means to be a Longhorn for Life, by sharing how Vince Young has come back to the University to work after his athletic career ended, and has also finished his degree, ten years after leaving school. And when he wants to help keep his "kids" safe, he might tell the story about how Cole Pittman, one of his players that tragically lost his life in a car accident, and the deep impact it had on the Longhorn program, and the Longhorn family, a group that now will always include Pittman's parents and family.

Some of the most powerful use of storytelling to reinforce cultural values can be seen at the safety-leading firms in construction and oil and gas industries. These are very large companies that employ hundreds of thousands of people, and put them onto jobsites that can be very dangerous. As such, creating a culture that supports and enforces a safe working environment is critical. Companies with consistently demonstrated safety cultures have significantly lower injury and fatality rates than ones that do not. But the data also supports my assertion of entropy above. If the leadership neglects to consistently reinforce safety culture, injury rates deteriorate quickly, and tragically.

So, the best safety cultures create constant reminders. In these types of companies, it is common to begin every meeting in every part of the company with a "safety moment". A "safety moment" is when a chosen leader will share a story that highlights some aspect of their safety culture; a story of how a worker avoided a dangerous accident by following procedures, or how someone saved a colleague from a near miss with a heroic effort, or tragically, perhaps how a co-worker was once tragically injured or died in a preventable situation. These stories act as a daily reminder that their business can be dangerous, and in their culture, nothing is more important than every worker going home to their family every night, healthy.

So, I would suggest that as a leader of your company's culture, you need to have your set of go-to stories that help you communicate your connection it. Moreover, you want to create simple visible and memorable images that help every employee that hears the story, understand how their behavior ends up affecting themselves, colleagues, customers, partners, and shareholders. That is in essence, the way leaders "teach" culture.

 Coaching Point: What may seem to begin as a symbolic gesture can often turn into enduring stories that help people communicate the culture for your organization. Design the stories you would like to see told and live that story.

But You Can't Go it Alone

But you cannot always be present to role model the culture for everyone or be available to tell a story at any given moment. And that is why having strong, clear expectations is so important. Urban Meyer shared in his book, "Culture is what leads when no one is watching". Ideally, everyone is pulling the culture forward together, but that discounts the truth of cultural "microclimates" within any large enterprise. Those pockets of culture occur due to both extrinsic and intrinsic factors affecting the group. To ensure a healthy alignment to culture in these pockets within the organization, you need other leaders in the organization to drive it. You will need ambassadors other than yourself, if the culture is going to be pervasive.

Who those ambassadors are is critical. To be effective, your cultural leaders must also be the most successful, and the highest overall performers. To be sustainable, your culture must be modeled by people that produce results, are rewarded for it, and ultimately, are respected by the rest of the organization. Without that, you will always be "pushing the rock uphill". However, if you are able to recruit those type of informal leaders in the organization, they will be your most powerful allies in transforming or reinforcing your desired culture.

When he was at the University of Florida, Meyer had one of those players in Tim Tebow. Tebow was a coach's dream. He was an amazing player on the field, winning the Heisman Trophy in 2007 to go along with the two national championships he won during his time at Florida. But while he was blessed with a rare level of athletic ability, he was also the hardest working player on the team. He lived in the weight room, and practiced at game-level intensity every day. As such, Tebow was an outstanding informal culture leader. He demonstrated alignment to Meyer's cultural blueprint, and proved that those behaviors were consistent with results on the football field, both as an individual player and for the whole team.

 Coaching Point: Your best performers must also be your most visible cultural ambassadors.

The 10-80-10 Paradigm

Meyer has a theory about his particular cultural expectations, which are centered around every member of the team giving an absolute maximum effort on every repetition in every practice. He calls it his 10-80-10 theory[50], and I believe it applies to business organizational culture as well. The theory is based on the idea that 10% of his players will be fully bought in, self-motivated, always give maximum effort, and consistently willing to put in the work to be outstanding players and team members. These are the players that produce on the field at the highest level, and simply must be willing to be cultural leaders for you as well if your culture is to be successful and sustainable. High performers that are getting results and rewarded are respected by the

. . . .

[50](Meyer U. , 2015)

rest of the organization and have the higher likelihood of encouraging others to model new behaviors.

Another 10% are exactly the opposite. Meyer suggests that they are likely to be talented players, but perhaps just not dedicated to excellence, not willing to put in the level of effort to take their performance to the next level, and as such, not willing to adhere to the behavioral expectations he has established. Meyer believes those players are not worthy of recruiting into the culture, as they will reject it, and may even actively try to undermine it.

For Meyer, the goal is the 80%. The 80% group are talented people that demonstrate their willingness to buy in to the culture, and often are fully engaged, but that they are missing an ingredient or simply the consistency of behavior to make it to the next level. Meyer believes that those players must be won over, one at a time. And he believes that the top 10% players are the keys to winning those players over. He intentionally pairs up players he knows are in the top 10% with players in the 80% group that he believes are on the edge, and have the potential to be top 10%ers. He described a simple example like that he would require top 10%ers to bring an 80%er with them to weight room to exercise during informal workouts. He felt if they saw what the top 10% did, they would be able to model it for themselves. So, with that 1:1 strategy, his goal is to simply move players into that top group every day.

This is an especially valuable approach for businesses that are going through some type of business or cultural transformation. Change is hard, and you will certainly have alignment from a select group of people who "get it". But, it will be important for you as a leader to find the individuals who both buy into your vision and culture, but are also high performers. Your job with them will be to convince them to join you in winning over the rest of the organization, actively recruiting from that next level pool of employees, to become another high-performing cultural ambassador. While you must lead and role model for the whole organization as well, I believe Meyer's suggested 1:1 approach is valuable, and undeniably impactful.

 Coaching Point: Culture is transformed one person at a time.

Maximizing your ROT (Return on Time)

That leaves you with the bottom 10%. Meyer explains his journey of learning about the bottom 10%. As a coach in his earlier years, he spent a significant portion of his time trying to coach these players, convincing them of the opportunity they have to step up and be great players. But like other leaders, he found that you cannot give someone motivation that they do not possess. You can fan a spark into a flame, but you cannot make fire where a spark does not exist.

Meyer's theory closely resembles a common human capital theory called the "Vitality Curve"[51]. It describes a theory that workforces are comprised of 20% top performers, 70% that make up the core of the workforce that do solid work, and the bottom 10% that are low performers. When he was at GE, Jack Welch embraced this model, labeling these groups as A, B, and C players, respectively. His approach was to disproportionately reward and make effort to retain A players, support, coach and encourage B players, and to do his best to remove C players, systematically. He described his approach in his seminal book, "Straight from the Gut"[52] which became the blueprint for organizations in pursuit of a "high performance culture". A lot of today's approach to employee compensation and talent development are still rooted in this fundamental approach. Management time, coaching, rewards and opportunities are focused on that top 20%, with a minimum level of resources applied to the rest of the organization. Re-

[51](Various, Vitality Curve, n.d.)
[52](Welch, 2003)

search shows that the top performers deliver a meaningfully higher level of production from the rest of the organization, so significant effort is applied to attract and retain them.

But I think businesses miss on Meyer's lesson of engaging, and perhaps expecting, top performers to be actively engaged in recruiting the next level of performer into the ranks of cultural leadership. And given the additional rewards they receive, it seems reasonable to expect their effort in building and expanding the reach of the desired organizational culture. The effective organizational culture leader has an expanding cadre of high performers that are actively working to add other high performers to their ranks, modeling the desired culture of the organization.

 Coaching Point: You cannot create or transform culture on your own. You need to cultivate a set of committed high-performers to win over the masses.

This is Your Stop, Time to Get Off the Bus

Business writers like Jim Collins talk about the importance of getting the "right people on the bus", which speaks of finding great team members to bring into the organization. But I would posit that it may be more important to "get the wrong people off the bus". In Meyer's world, the bottom 10% waste some coaching time, and take a spot that could be available for a more willing player. But those bottom 10%ers likely never see the field, so their impact is lessened. Those bottom performers are probably much more caustic to your organization and the culture you are trying to build.

In my work as a consultant, I work with cross-sections of company leaders for a broad array of Fortune 500 companies. Within every group, you see this type of clustering; a small group of people who are highly engaged to the company's vision, purpose and strategy, and motivated to see it succeed, a large middle group that are very capable, yet still have some type of reticence towards, or lack of understanding of, the company's direction to fully engage, and another small group that seems hell bent on undermining the desired culture of the organization. And in those settings, what I see is a battle for the hearts and minds of the middle group. Both the highly engaged and actively disengaged groups want people to join their ranks. The middle group intrinsically wants to buy in – you can see it in their faces. But for most people, the human psyche is quite frail. Doubt creeps in easily. The negative energy that the bottom group exudes is powerful, and it springs from a seemingly limitless energy source. To combat it you need to balance it with energy from your top performers. And sadly, you will need to systematically remove the people that will not, or cannot align to, or are actively undermining your organizational culture.

 Coaching Point: There are people in your organization that are actively and systematically undermining your desired culture. You may find more success in removing them from the organization, rather than trying to turn them around.

CHALK TALK
DEPLOYING YOUR CULTURE

Culture must be actively led

- Culture starts with Leadership. Leadership > Culture > Behavior > Results and it cannot be

- Culture will slide into disorder without active leadership

- Strong cultures are created by very visible demonstrations of what is valued and what will not be tolerated

Tell Stories

- Those visible exhibitions of leadership will form the stories that will carry on the culture

- Culture, and those stories are what leads when no one else is looking
- Be proactive in creating and sharing your culture leadership anecdotes

Engage Others Strategically

- You can't do it all – you need to engage others to help you proliferate and sustain your desired culture
- Create safe vehicles for self-policing, but never abdicate your role as the leader of culture
- To be effective, your culture ambassadors should also be your highest performers
- Your culture is perceived differently by the A, B, and C players in your organization, and your focus must be on the B group, with support from the A group
- Your cultural C group are likely actively undermining your desired culture, and if true, they are having an outsized negative impact on your culture
- Be proactive, and encourage the C cultural group to leave the company – they are toxic

GAME PLAN

CULTURE

So, in summary, organizations have cultures; planned or unplanned, positive or negative, aligned or misaligned with its corporate goals. The culture you actually have is a product of what you have designed and communicated, how clearly it is defined, whether leaders in the organization actually demonstrate the defined behaviors, and what behaviors outside of your definition you actually tolerate. The effectiveness and sustainability of that culture is dependent upon how you deploy it; whether you demonstrably lead it, and how you engage others to role model it, and to pull others in with them.

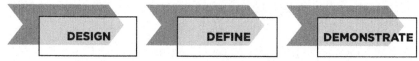

FIGURE 23. ORGANIZATIONAL CULTURE PROCESS

PRE-GAME

Design

Find your recipe for the organizational culture that will be most effective for your organization. Prioritize each statement from 1-4, with 4 reflecting the statement that is most consistent with your perspective of what would be most effective for your organization.

Desired State Culture

1. Vision	Priority
A. We want to be the employer of choice and considered one of the best places to work in our industry	
B. We want to be the very best at what we do	
C. We want to be #1 in our market	
D. We want to be the partner of choice, and the most connected company in our space	

2. Results Focus	Priority
A. We want to attract and retain the best talent in the industry	
B. We want to have the highest quality of products and services	
C. We want to the highest customer loyalty in our industry	
D. We want to have the highest growth	

3. We measure success by...	Priority
A. Productivity	
B. Quality	
C. Market Share	
D. Revenue or Customer Growth	

4. We need leaders who...	Priority
A. Are good delegators and empower others	
B. Are detail-oriented and drive continuous improvement	
C. Are competitive and have a winning mindset	
D. Are inclusive and inspire others	

5. Our industry can be best be characterized as...	Priority
A. Productivity	
B. Quality	
C. Market Share	
D. Revenue or Customer Growth	

6. For us to be successful, the most powerful function would need to be...	Priority
A. Shared Services – HR, IT, Legal, Finance	
B. Manufacturing or Product/Service Development	
C. Sales	
D. Marketing	

Add up all of the priority numbers associated with each letter, and enter in the boxes below.

A	B	C	D

Here is an example wherein answer "A" was the highest prioritized answer on every question, followed by B, C and D, in that order.

A	B	C	D
24	18	12	6

Now, answer the questions below using the same approach as above. But, for this section, select the option that best represents what you actually see at your organization today.

Current State

1. We are most proud about our...	Priority
A. culture	
B. products and services	
C. financial performance	
D. relationship with customers and partners	

2. We spend most of our time in meetings discussing...	Priority
A. Talent acquisition, development and retention	
B. Operational KPIs	
C. Customer feedback	
D. The value we create in the market	

3. What gets rewarded around here	Priority
A. Collaborating across the organization	
B. Hitting goals consistently	
C. Financial performance	
D. Landing a new customer or partner	

4. Leaders who get promoted tend to be...	Priority
A. Great collaborators and coaches	
B. Operationally sound and expert at their function	
C. Competitive and hard charging	
D. Industry gurus who are thought leaders	

5. When we talk about innovation, we tend to think about breakthrough...	Priority
A. Ways to deliver value through people	
B. Process improvements that drive higher quality or performance	
C. Customer insights that enable new products or services	
D. Business models that transform the industry	

6.	The organization that calls the shots around here is...	Priority
A.	Shared Services – HR, IT, Legal, Finance	
B.	Manufacturing or Product/Service Development	
C.	Sales	
D.	Marketing	

Again, add all of the prioritization numbers associated with each letter and add them to the table below.

So, if you imagined a situation that was the opposite of the example provided in the Desired State example, wherein the highest prioritization was always on D, followed by C, B, and A, respectively, then you would have a set of data that looks like this (when added to the Desired State):

	A	B	C	D
Desired State	24	18	12	6
Current State	6	12	18	24

When you plot these on a spider chart as below, it highlights the gaps between your Desired Culture, and your Current Culture.

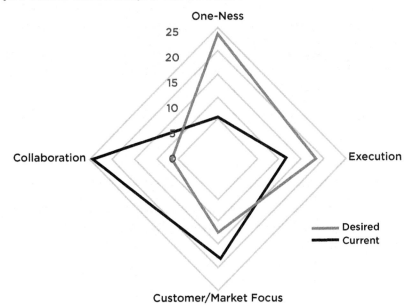

FIGURE 24. EXAMPLE CULTURE SPIDER CHART

GAME TIME

Define

Detail the key behaviors that define your Desired Culture, and the behaviors that will not be tolerated. To inspire you, consider:

- *Vision.* What type of behavior is consistent with bringing that vision to life?

- *Values.* In what situations will they be called into question? How do you want your people to show up in those moments?

- *Purpose.* What behaviors are consistent with us fulfilling our organizational Purpose?

- *Strategy.* What kind of activities are central to your strategy? What does great strategic execution look like in those moments?

- *Business Model.* What activities are fundamental to how we generate business outcomes? What metrics are we focused on? What activities or behaviors are consistent with strong performance in those areas?

- *Organizational structure.* How do we need to relate to one another to be most effective?

- *Key function.* How should the organization support our key function?

- *Stakeholders.* How should we relate to our broader set of stakeholders such as customers, partners and shareholders?

- *Leadership style.* What type of leader will be most effective for our desired culture? What does that type of leadership look like in action?

DESIRED BEHAVIORS	
Company Value or Cultural Aspect	Description of Desired Behavior

PROHIBITED BEHAVIORS	
Company Value or Cultural Aspect	Description of Prohibited Behavior

POST-GAME

Deploy

Once you have created your list key cultural behaviors, and those that are prohibited, rate the organization on well it demonstrates and avoids those behaviors, respectively.

Write in the behavior and circle that frequency that best characterizes how often employees demonstrate that desired behavior.

DESIRED BEHAVIOR			
Infrequently	Somewhat Infrequently	Somewhat Frequently	Frequently
Infrequently	Somewhat Infrequently	Somewhat Frequently	Frequently
Infrequently	Somewhat Infrequently	Somewhat Frequently	Frequently
Infrequently	Somewhat Infrequently	Somewhat Frequently	Frequently
Infrequently	Somewhat Infrequently	Somewhat Frequently	Frequently

Write in the prohibited behavior and circle that frequency that best characterizes how often employees display that desired behavior.

PROHIBITED BEHAVIOR			
Often	Occasionally	Somewhat Seldom	Seldom
Often	Occasionally	Somewhat Seldom	Seldom
Often	Occasionally	Somewhat Seldom	Seldom
Often	Occasionally	Somewhat Seldom	Seldom
Often	Occasionally	Somewhat Seldom	Seldom

- What are the biggest gaps with respect to the Desired Behaviors?
- What risks are present due to the exhibition of some of the Prohibited Behaviors?

- What should you Stop/Start/Do More/Do Less within the company to help close these gaps and mitigate these risks?

Leading the Culture.

- What are the most important cultural messages you need to send to the organization?

- How could you address your known gaps?

- What are the stories you need to tell?

- Who are your current cultural ambassadors? Who would you want them to recruit?

- Do you know of any large scale cultural diminishers? Can you move them out of the organization?

SECTION IV

PULLING IT ALL TOGETHER
INTEGRATING YOUR SYSTEM

INTEGRATING VISION, STRATEGY & CULTURE

The Steeler Way

1970 was a watershed year for the NFL. It marked the merger of the old NFL with the AFL, and the formation of the NFL as it is today, and essentially the beginning of the modern era of professional football. Nearly all modern statistics in the NFL use this date as the first date of measurement.

That year was also an important year for the Pittsburgh Steelers. It was the first year of Three Rivers Stadium, the home for the Steelers for the next 30 years, where they won 5 conference titles. It was also the year that they drafted Terry Bradshaw with the #1 overall pick in the draft, who quarterbacked them to 4 Super Bowl titles, winning Super Bowl MVP twice.

Since that year, covering the entire modern era of the NFL, the Pittsburgh Steelers have been the most successful team in the league. They have won more division championships (21) and Super Bowl championships (6) than any other team, and have won more regular season games since the merger, by a wide margin[53]. What is the se-

. . . .

[53](Various, Composite NFL records since the AFL merged into the NFL in 1970, n.d.)

cret to their success? I would argue that quite consciously, they have created, installed, and maintained an integrated system, where their Vision, Strategy & Culture are aligned and mutually reinforcing.

Dan Rooney (1932-2017), is the son of the original owner of the Steelers, Art Rooney, Sr. During his tenure as president of the Steelers, he established the Vision for the Steelers organization, which was to "represent the city of Pittsburgh in the National Football League, primarily by winning the championship of professional football". So, by simply reading the statement, you can discern that aside from winning games, they intend to stand up and represent the city of Pittsburgh[54].

A Pittsburgh Guy, a Steeler Guy

The Rooney family has been in the city of Pittsburgh for generations, and as Irish immigrants, they identify closely with the working class history of the city, and authentically understand and align to the values of humbleness, hard work, fairness, and kindness that have long characterized the city. So, to "represent the city" and "win championships", and do so in an integrated way, they were going to have to ensure that the way the team operated and played would reflect the soul of the city. I think it is fair to say that they have been successful in that endeavor. The team has always demonstrated a reputation as humble, hard-working winners, supported by similar fans in what has been characterized as a classic "rust belt" city built on the values of honest, hardworking, genuine people.

That hardworking approach is reflected in the organization's strategy around offensive and defensive philosophy as well. Through most of its history, the Steelers have been known for a strong, aggressive defense, and sound, fundamental offensive football, built around a

[54](Staff, 2011)

conservative rushing attack. The data supports that perceived identity. Statistically, the Steelers have been the best defensive team since
the merger[55]. This approach reinforced the connection to the city,
and helped create the deep bonds they have with the fan base. A fi-
nesse-oriented team with a soft defense would have never been popular in Pittsburgh. The commitment to fundamentals is also a Steeler
trademark initiated by coach Chuck Noll, and perpetuated by the two
coaches that have followed him.

Their Vision specifically embraced the purpose of serving their community and contributing to the advancement of all people in that
community. As an organization that is built by and run by Pittsburgh
people, it is only natural that they would serve the local community,
and the Steelers have done so. The Steelers support many local char-
ities with funds, as well as their time in working on charity projects
and of course, personal appearances by the players. Their success on
the field has helped them raise more money for charity, and only en-
hanced their standing in the community.

Art Rooney, Sr. set the standard for a loyalty to individuals. In the
late 60's, the Steelers drafted Rocky Bleier with a 16th round pick out
of Notre Dame – nearly an afterthought. But, Bleier impressed team
leaders with his relentless work ethic, and he beat the odds and made
the team. Soon after, he was drafted into the Army and sent to Viet-
nam, where he sustained a serious injury to his foot. Given the nature
and extent of his injury, he was not expected to walk fully normally
again, and his doctors informed him that he should give up the notion
of ever playing football again.

But upon his completion of his military service, he was invited back
to the Steelers. Rooney, kept him on the practice squad and made all
the team's resources – doctors, facilities, etc. – available to Bleier…

. . . .

[55](Various, Composite NFL records since the AFL merged into the NFL in 1970, n.d.)

for four years! Out respect for his military service, and his unyielding attitude – clearly a "Steeler Guy", Rooney never lost faith in him, and was rewarded with a valuable player that became a crucial part of the Steelers' dynasty of the 1970's.

Dan Rooney continued his father's commitment to fairness to individuals as well. He is the author of what is now known as the "Rooney Rule", which requires all NFL clubs to at least interview minority coaching and front office candidates to ensure fair and honest hiring practices.

That commitment to the individual shows up in the makeup of the rest of the team as well. The Steelers have always demonstrated a commitment to building the team through the draft, as opposed to free agency. As much as talent, they are looking for more "Pittsburgh guys" that reflect the values that the organization stands for. They fiercely avoid bad actors, or "low character" players, and do not hesitate to release players that have demonstrated behaviors that are not consistent with the Steeler culture. By building through the draft, they tend to have players in their organization longer, and demonstrate a commitment to individuals growing, developing and earning their starting positions. As such, players tend to live in the city longer, so more players end up making Pittsburgh their permanent home after they retire.

The level of permanency extends to the coaching staff and the front office. The Rooney family instills loyalty into the organizational culture, by visibly sticking by coaches, even after a few subpar seasons. The Steelers have only had three coaches since 1969, a level of permanence and stability that no other team is even marginally close to. While the Steelers' last three coaches have covered 48 years, the next closest team chimes in at only half that, and the average is about one quarter of that. And as for the front office, the Rooney family has maintained ownership and management of the club since it was purchased in 1933.

That family presence extends beyond the front office. If you utilize the culture framework I introduced earlier, the Steelers clearly bias towards the One-ness culture, where alignment is the dominant characteristic. That includes an alignment to the personal character modeled and actively led by the Rooney family, alignment to the family atmosphere they perpetuate within the entire organization, alignment to the commitment to the community, alignment to the humble identity and genuine character of that community, and the commitment to hard work, supporting each other, excellence in fundamentals, and the sacrifice required to consistently play at a championship level.

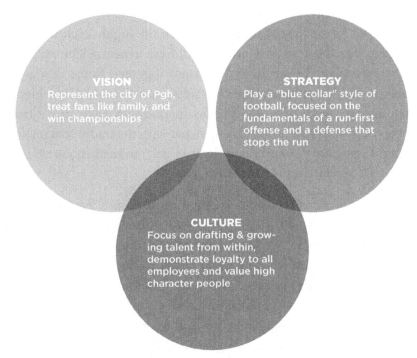

FIGURE 25. PITTSBURGH STEELERS' INTEGRATED SYSTEM

The Steelers have a consistent formula that has created a clear brand that Pittsburgh fans can identify with and trust. No other team draws as many fans in the opposing teams' stadiums – Steeler Nation is everywhere. And that brand identity has created financial stability for the organization, as evidenced by the epically long waiting list for season tickets. But despite the overwhelming demand for tickets, the Steelers average season ticket price is in the lower half of the NFL – reinforcing the Rooney family's commitment to fairness to the community. When your Vision, Strategy and Culture are integrated, and fully aligned, you create a flywheel of performance, that drives sustained excellence.

The Southwest Way

Southwest Airlines has been the Pittsburgh Steelers of the airline industry. They have been profitable for 44 straight years, a record of consistency that is nearly unfathomable in the highly cyclical airline industry. During long stretches, Southwest generated more profit than the rest of the airline industry put together. Since they went public in 1977, Southwest has generated returns roughly 50% higher than the broader market. During that period they have grown from being the upstart to a major player, on par with the traditional majors. Again, I attribute this success, at least in part, to their integrated approach to Vision, Strategy and Culture.

The origin of all of this value creation can famously be traced back to a drawing on a napkin in a bar in San Antonio. Two men had a vision for what would become Southwest Airlines, a vision to bring the convenience and freedom of air travel to more people. In 1967 when Southwest was formed, only a small percentage of Americans had flown commercially, and far fewer did so on a regular basis. Herb Kelleher and Rollin King had a vision to democratize the skies. They had a Vision, but they were going to need a strategy.

To deliver on that Vision, they were going to radically lower fares. They felt they could do that by only using one type of plane – minimizing maintenance fees, and flying in and out of secondary airports, to reduce gate and hangar fees. But that was not enough. To make up for the lower price, they were going to need to have volume, and higher utilization of each plane - they were going to have to fly more flights per day per plane. At first, that simply meant having a tightly focused route structure – essentially a triangle defined by San Antonio, Dallas and Houston.

Everyone Needs to Pitch in

But that would not be enough. To get the volume they needed, they were going to have to push through the accepted barriers of turn time between each flight. In the early 1970's, the average turn time for a traditional airline was nearly an hour. To make their model work, Southwest knew it was going to need to be radically lower, setting a target of 10 minutes! To pull that off, they were going to have to have a significant level of collaboration from all operations personnel; gate agents, flight attendants, baggage handlers, catering, even pilots. But that is easier said than done. In traditional airlines, several of these groups are represented by entirely different unions, each with their own very prescriptive takes on job descriptions. This created a very bureaucratic culture, and to be successful, Southwest was going to need a very different type of culture.

Southwest was going to need to create an environment that encouraged and enabled collaboration from a broad set of stakeholders. Gate agents were going to need to help with luggage, baggage was going to have to help catering turn the food and beverage carts, flight attendants, and even pilots, where going to have to help clean the cabin to make this quick turn approach happen.

Moreover, they were going to have get collaboration from customers. The traditional assigned seating approach had proven to be an obstacle, and they were going to need to convince customers to accept open seating, on a first come, first serve basis. They were also going to have to manage their own luggage more.

To bring this all together, and make it sustainable, they were going to have to make it fun somehow. So, quite intentionally, they instilled a light-hearted atmosphere onboard. The flat structure and egalitarian feel created a "we are all in this together" atmosphere that made passengers feel like they were part of the action, that it was just transportation, and that flying with Southwest could be fun. Southwest was going to need a special kind of employee. They needed people who were hard-working, but also ones that laugh with others, and sometimes, at themselves. The commitment to the customer experience was serious, but the experience itself did not need to be.

Fifty years later, the environment around air travel, especially post-9/11, has changed, and Southwest has grown far beyond the Texas Triangle, but their unique recipe of Vision, Strategy and Culture has lived on. And it has created a level of sustained success with no peers in the industry. As aforementioned, Southwest has outperformed every other airline over its history, and in several years, it has outperformed the entire industry all by itself. And I believe you can attribute that success to a very elegant integrated system.

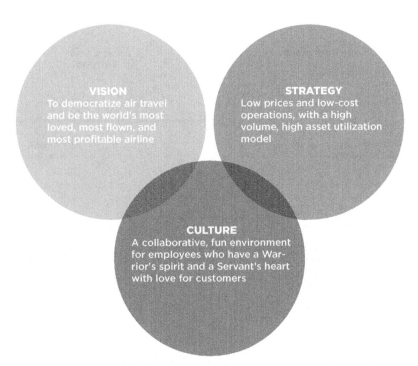

FIGURE 26. SOUTHWEST AIRLINES' INTEGRATED SYSTEM

A Bold Vision

Standing back from this integrated system, you can quickly see the elegance of how perfectly each element of Vision, Strategy & Culture mutually reinforce each other. But first, let's look at each one separately first.

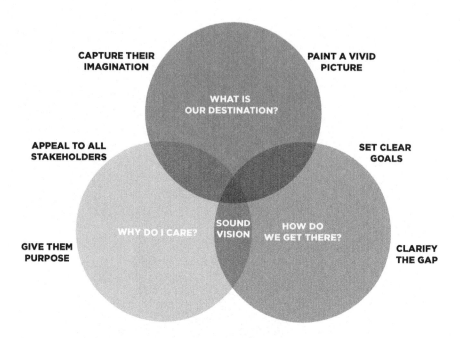

When you look at Southwest's Vision through the lens of the framework in this book, you can see how they leveraged all of the key elements describing a great vision:

- *They set a clear destination.* They captured people's imagination about what air travel could be. That it could be fun – that you would love to travel, and that the people working there might love their job. And that in the midst of that fun, they were going to run a great business and make a lot of money for shareholders.

- *They showed you the path.* They set clear, measurable goals – they were going to be the most loved (highest customer satisfaction ratings), most flown (most segments per plane), and most profitable airline (profit per seat-mile). They clarified the gap – they would need to turn planes faster than anyone in the industry, and to do that everyone was going to pitch in.

- *They brought the LUV.* They had a Purpose – to democratize the skies, to make air travel accessible to everyone. And they included everyone in that vision; customers, gate agents, flight attendants, baggage handlers, pilots, and customer service agents. Everyone was part of the Vision, and everyone had a part to play.

Disruptive Strategy

They had a sound Vision, and it was simple - Simple to communicate, simple to understand, and simple to follow. But they would need a sound strategy as well. As a startup, planning to compete against established competitors, with strong incumbent positions, they were clearly operating from a position of weakness. They had the planes, the international coverage, the access to the gates at the major airports, and the prestige and brand cache. They were going to need to innovate.

As such, they challenged accepted truths:

Accepted Truth	Challenging that Truth
Airlines must have national or international coverage to be relevant	They could establish themselves as a regional player, but with scale
They would need a broad set of aircraft	They could standardize on one kind of aircraft, especially since they were going to running all regional routes
People would only want to fly from the major airports	Flying from secondary airports could offer an attractive alternative to the major ones
Air travel was expensive	There was an opportunity for a low cost airline
Airlines were for wealthy individuals or business fliers	Air travel was for everyone

FIGURE 27. SOUTHWEST CHALLENGE OF ACCEPTED TRUTHS

But to challenge those truths, they had to carefully ask themselves, "What Would Have to Be True?" if they were upended. Just a few of them:

- If they were going to have low prices, they were going to have to have a lower cost significantly lower cost structure.

- If they were going to have low prices, they were going to have to have higher volume.

- If they were going to have higher volume, they were going to have to turn planes faster

But, going through this exercise convinced them that while they were in a position of weakness, relative to the established major airlines, there were clearly opportunities:

- In their effort to create a scalable hub and spoke architecture, the major airlines had created a system where more often than not, you were navigating through their respective hub airports

- This complex network of flights required a very complicated reservation system that necessitated a complicated inventory system and a network of travel agents available for customers

- Their broad assortment of travel distances favored a broad assortment of aircraft that would optimally match the haul length for cost purposes

- Their traditional set of unionized employees made collaboration across functions difficult

- That broad set of unionized employees, combined with extensive gate access at the premier airports, and the commissions required by the travel agents inflated the major airlines' cost structure

That combination of starting from a position of weakness relative to its competitors, and an attractive set of opportunities led them to a set of Tackling Strategies, like we described in the Strategy section:

TACKLING STRATEGIES Actively pursue opportunities to counteract your weakness and change the game	
Innovate to minimize weaknesses	Their unique approach to getting all of their key stakeholders to dramatically change their turn time may have been their most powerful innovation
Poach Talent	Southwest's success and growth required a lot of talent acquisition, and that success, as well as their fun and upbeat culture attracted people with that mindset, and enticed many to move away from the majors.
Invest surgically to address weaknesses	They invested in aircraft very surgically – only 737s, often used aircraft from other airlines
Aggressively pursue regulatory change	Dallas was a part of their strategy from the very beginning as the move from Love Field to DFW was going to leave Dallas without an airport with a major airline serving it. In an attempt to protect the investment in DFW, the state legislature enacted the Wright Amendment[56], aimed at limiting air travel from Love Field to only regional travel. Southwest actively lobbied for the amendment's repeal for years, only recently finding success. But that battle framed up the issue as anti-competitive, and Southwest Airlines as the hero, fighting for the rights of everyday citizens – their adopted customer base whom the majors had alienated.

[56](Various, History of Southwest Airlines, n.d.)

Pursue customers with a sharp focus	Southwest had a very clear message – Low Prices Everyday. They were maniacal about simplicity – low fares from a central reservation system, open seating, just drinks and peanuts on the flight. It was clearly appealing to people who commuted frequently within the network, and to those people that were new to flying – the key customer segments that they focused on.
Use classic problem-solving techniques to create solutions	Translating the Opportunities into a cohesive strategy requires creativity and solid problem-solving skills and techniques
Don't get pessimistic	Being the upstart within an industry is not easy. You are often portrayed by incumbents as a joke or a pest that should be ignored. Southwest's choice of culture had clear strategic value, but also was a key to their resiliency in the face of tough execution challenges

FIGURE 28. SOUTHWEST'S TACKLING STRATEGIES

The goal of Tackling strategies is to "tackle" opportunities, and to "change the game". Clearly, Southwest's strategy was made possible by their commitment to questioning accepted "rules" of the airline industry, uncovering opportunities left behind by the majors, and fundamentally changing the common airline business model. Moreover, they changed the way an airline branded itself, and the customer experience airlines traditionally offered.

That strategy was built on the Industrial Organization Model for Above Average Returns, a framework based several key elements about the airline industry;

- The industry and competitive environment impose pressures and constraints and requires a strategy to overcome them to create above average returns. Clearly the airline industry and its heavy regulation, restricted access to gates at major airports, a unified inventory system, creates significant challenges to incumbents. Those constraints limit competition, and can dilute the competitiveness and responsiveness of incumbents, making them ripe for disruption of the type presented by Southwest.

- Many firms competing in that industry have access to similar resources and thus may pursue similar strategies. As a regulated industry with employees from within the same unions, and flying planes made by the same manufacturers, and all using a common inventory system, all players clearly have access to similar resources and pursue common strategies. Again, given the lack of differentiation within that group, Southwest represented a truly unique alternative that offered a very real choice for the market and a threat to the incumbents.

- Resources used by firms are highly mobile across firms. Southwest was actually buying some used planes from the majors, and recruited pilots, attendants, baggage handles, etc. from the same acquisition pools. And again, Southwest represented a differentiated choice for industry talent.

LUV Culture

Clearly, they designed a powerful strategy that clearly delivered Above Average Returns. So, with a compelling strategy mapped out, they were going to need a Culture to facilitate it, power it, and sustain it. Given their very externally-focused strategy, and the fact that they were not using unique internal assets, they would need a culture that was externally focused as well. Now in their early years as a business, their success was going to be highly dependent upon getting buy-in from both external labor pools and new hires, and acquiring customers that were new to the air travel, I would characterize their optimal culture at that time to be most like a Collaboration archetype.

COLLABORATION CULTURE	
Leadership Attributes	
Inclusive Leadership Style	Herb Kelleher was often described as an empathetic leader[57], who focused more on hiring the right people, and then letting them lead. Given the wide range of stakeholders that he depended upon, and how much alignment he needed from them, it would be critical for them to feel fully included in the vision for the company.
Inspiring Leadership Personality Profile	The Collaboration archetype often relies on an Inspiring leader personality profile, and given the change he was driving, it would be critical for Kelleher to be able to communicate a vision, and build faith and dedication into his employees.
Managerial Focus – Stakeholder Management	The Collaboration culture requires significant focus on Stakeholder Management. For the strategy to work, Southwest was going to need commitment and execution from a broad range of stakeholders as described above; internal ones like pilots, flight attendants, baggage handlers, as well as external stakeholders such as legislators, regulators, union representatives, and even customers.

[57](Gaille, 2013)

Key Skill - Influence	Since Southwest would be counting on the support of such a broad range of stakeholders that were outside of their direct control, leaders at the company were going to require strong skills in leading without formal authority, and externally-facing employees would need the ability to successfully influence others to support the Vision.
Example Leader – Mack Brown	Mack Brown and Herb Kelleher have a lot of similar traits. While Kelleher was likely more gregarious than Brown, both were excellent at connecting with their stakeholders, and creating a sense of loyalty that transcending the business or management transaction.
Business Attributes	
Market Stage – Early Growth	While the air travel industry was already past the early growth phase, Southwest was introducing a major disruption, and a very different business model than the majors, essentially creating a new market segment.
Key Metric – Revenue Growth	In an Early Growth phase like Southwest had created with their new business model, your biggest proof point is your ability to lure customers. So, Revenue Growth is the simplest way to measure whether your new business model is generating success.

Innovation Focus – Disruptive Business Model	As discussed here, the underlying purpose of a Collaboration culture is to nurture relationships across a broad set of stakeholders to do something very radically different. In many cases, this organizational culture archetype is there to support the effort of creating an entirely new business model, like what Southwest did to the air travel industry.
Striving for – New Ground	Southwest was challenging not only a concept of route design, but a complete mindset shift around the customer experience. In succeeding, they created a new category – the discount airline.
Fascinated by - Relationships	Southwest redefined the company's relationship with its employees relative to traditional carriers, as well as the air travel customer, creating a more personal connection than any of their predecessors.

FIGURE 29. SOUTHWEST'S LUV CULTURE

When people talk about the success of Southwest Airlines, they often point to the unique culture and brand of the company – how their people seem to be having fun while doing their job, the environment they create for their customers, their somewhat irreverent marketing, etc. They are amazingly powerful and consistent, and have been a significant part of their success.

But, those things are just what customers and the general public can see most easily. Without the clear and compelling vision, and without the fully integrated strategy, there is no magic – and I feel confident in saying this – they would have not only not thrived, they would not have even survived.

GAME PLAN

INTEGRATING YOUR SYSTEM

So, how do you create and install your own system? Given the interconnected nature of this systematic approach, where do you begin? Consider this simple step by step approach:

1. **Begin with the Customer.** Who is your customer? Be very specific of your description of the customer – this is not time for generalities. Once you have a clear picture of a customer that you want to pursue, identify the problem you want to solve for them. There are great books out there on creating unique customer insights, and validating real pain that customers will want to pay someone to resolve for them. If this is not a comfort zone for you, then I recommend you get smart on that process, and while you may want to hire someone to help you, you can cannot contract this out to someone. This first step is important, and you have to understand these insights intimately. Work with only one customer problem at a time. This is the focus of your system.

2. **Devise a Strategy to Resolve the Problem.** Using the tools I have provided, and your unique business model and approach to products and services, devise a solution to that unique customer's specific problem. Again, this is not your entire strategy, this is simply your strategy to solve that customer problem. This is the "What" of your system.

3. **Design the Culture You Will Need to Deliver That Strategy.** What are the attributes of your industry and business model? What type of behaviors will you need from your employees and partners to successfully deliver on that strategy? What passions will your people have to have, and what type of leadership will you need to make those behaviors effective and sustainable? This is the "How" of your system.

4. **Develop a Vision That Will Influence Stakeholders to join you on the journey.** Using the tools provided earlier, write the story that would make customers believe that you could solve their problem, and compelling enough for other stakeholders to want to help you in the cause. Again, this is not your entire Vision, just what supports the Strategy and Culture you have created to address this customer need.

5. **Rinse, Repeat.** Repeat this process with the other specific customer needs you have identified, following this loop all the way around. Combine your Vision, Strategy, Culture elements, and consider them in their groups. In this way, by building an organizational system from the ground up, you ensure that the models, statements, and goals you create are based upon the core drivers of success for the business – not the other way around - and that all of the models are mutually reinforcing.

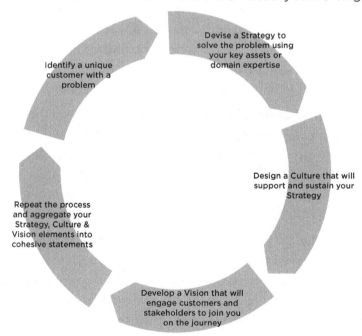

FIGURE 30. PROCESS TO CREATE AN INTEGRATED SYSTEM OF VISION, STRATEGY & CULTURE

Hopefully, I have reinforced or deepened your appreciation for the importance of having an integrated system that will provide you with a fundamentally sound foundation upon which to build your organization or team.

"Average leaders have a quote. Good leaders have a plan. Great leaders have a system."

—Urban Meyer, Head Coach, Ohio State Buckeyes

In this book, I have laid out a blueprint for how to create a system for your team or organization. An integrated system of Vision, Strategy and Culture gives you the best opportunity to win every battle you will fight.

"Every battle is won or lost before it is ever fought"

—Sun Tzu, Chinese military strategist and philosopher

And while Sun Tzu was not a football coach, his quote about preparation and getting Ahead of the Chains is the only sign hanging in the New England Patriots locker room.

THE END

COMING UP NEXT

Ahead of the Chains – Executing Your System

This book will focus on how to execute your system:

- *Execution*. I will focus on Coach Vince Lombardi, and develop insights into the nature of execution, and how having a clear "bread and butter play" can create the foundation for operational excellence. I will also present a framework and tools around driving execution by developing Competence through the rigor of practice, and building Confidence through leadership.

- *Talent*. The game of football is about specialization; finding the right talent with the competencies to execute your system. I will reflect on how the college game can inform our concepts around recruiting talent, while the NFL can provide insights on how we evaluate it. I will introduce a unique framework and set of tools for coaching talent, that is inspired by the best coaches in the game including Bill Walsh. Finally, leaning on the integrated system you have installed, I will discuss the criticality of attracting and retaining talent that is aligned to the culture you need for success

- *Leadership*. Through the eyes of several prominent football coaches, I will explore the value of leadership, and dig deeper into the role of a leader of an organization. Again, supporting your integrated system, I will introduce tools to help you understand yourself as a leader, and how you can best serve your organization. Finally, I close by exploring the nature of succession, recruiting and growing future leaders, and how you will create your leadership legacy.

I hope you enjoyed this volume enough to make you curious for the next one. Until then, I will sign off by reminding you to "Play hard, and play to the whistle".

Matt

WORKS CITED

Airlines, S. (Perpetual). *Southwest.com*. Retrieved from Southwest Airlines - Purpose, Vision, Values, and Mission: http://investors.southwest.com/our-company/purpose-vision-values-and-mission

Babers, D. (2015, December 15). *Syracuse football coach Dino Babers describes vision for team (video)*. Retrieved from Syracuse.com: http://www.syracuse.com/orangefootball/index.ssf/2015/12/dino_babers_syracuse_football_carrier_dome.html

Bailey, S. (2015, December 5). *http://www.syracuse.com/orangefootball/index.ssf/2015/12/dino_babers_syracuse_football_coach_national_media_expert_opinions.html*. Retrieved from Syracuse.com: http://www.syracuse.com/orangefootball/index.ssf/2015/12/dino_babers_syracuse_football_coach_national_media_expert_opinions.html

Balakrishnan, A. (2017, April 25). *Scandals may have knocked $10 billion off Uber's value, a report says.* Retrieved from cnbc.com: http://www.cnbc.com/2017/04/25/uber-stock-price-drops-amid-sexism-investigation-greyballing-and-apple-run-in--the-information.html

Barney, J., & Hesterly, W. (2011). *Strategic Management & Competitive Advantage.* Prentice Hall.

Bloom, P., & Kotler, P. (1975). Strategies for High Market Share Companies. *Harvard Business Review*.

Brown, C. (2013, December 14). *Mack Brown steps down after 16 years.* Retrieved from Rivals.com: https://texas.rivals.com/content.asp?CID=1585894

Brown, M. (2001). *One Heartbeat.* Albany, TX: Bright Sky Press.

Brown, M. (2006, January 4). *Texas Locker Room after '06 Rose Bowl win vs USC*. Retrieved from YouTube: https://www.youtube.com/watch?v=rvpI2HJkL34

Cantor, G. (2008). *Paul Brown: The Man Who Invented Modern Football.* Triumph Books.

Carroll, L. (1865). *Alice in Wonderland.*

Carson, B. (2017, March 4). *Uber's unraveling: The stunning, 2 week string of blows that has upended the world's most valuable startup.* Retrieved from Business Insider: http://www.businessinsider.com/uber-scandal-recap-2017-3?r=UK&IR=T/#wednesday-february-22-cocaine-and-groping-2

Cases, L. (2015). *The Management Ideas of Nick Saban.*

Charan, R. (2006, April). *Home Depot's Blueprint for Culture Change.* Retrieved from Harvard Business Review: https://hbr.org/2006/04/home-depots-blueprint-for-culture-change

Chettri, R. (2013). *Nike: a case study in change and management.* Retrieved from Academia.edu: https://www.academia.edu/7078862/Nike_a_case_study_in_change_and_management

Christopherson, B. (2007, October 27). *Texas is a shining example of a program turning itself around.* Retrieved November 2, 2013, from Husker Extra: http://journalstar.com/sports/huskers/football/texas-is-shining-example-of-a-program-turning-itself-around/article_bfcd2ed9-6ffc-5043-b75a-dbbe740a18ea.html

Collins, J. (2001). *Good to Great: Why Some Companies Make the Leap...and Others Don't.* New York: Harpers Business.

Cook, T. (2011, May 11). *Tim Cook's First Speech.* Retrieved from YouTube: https://www.youtube.com/watch?v=B52ENcthsb8

Cooper, J. (2014). *Nick Saban finally speaks out on NCAA's 10-second proposal.* Retrieved from Saturday Down South.

De La Merced, M. J. (2011, December 11). AT&T Ends $39 Billion Bid for T-Mobile. *New York Times.*

Finger, M. (2016, January 3). T*en Years Later, A Championship Speech Resonates.* Retrieved from San Antonio Express News: http://www.expressnews.com/sports/college_sports/longhorns/article/Ten-years-later-a-championship-speech-resonates-6734219.php

Forbes. (2010, March). The World's Billionaires. *Forbes.*

Gaille, B. (2013, October 15). *Southwest Airline's Herb Kelleher's Leadership Style.* Retrieved from Brandon Gaille: https://brandongaille.com/southwest-airlines-herb-kellehers-leadership-style/

Gallo, C. (2014, May 16). *Steve Jobs and Alan Mulally Unleashed Innovation With Two Simple Words.* Retrieved from Forbes: https://www.forbes.com/sites/carminegallo/2014/05/16/steve-jobs-and-alan-mulally-unleashed-innovation-with-two-simple-words/#78f1289c6275

Gates, B. (1995). *The Road Ahead.* Viking.

Gerdeman, T. (2015, August 25). *For Ohio State Nine Units Strong is the Goal, Everything Else is Inertia.* Retrieved from The O-Zone: http://theozone.net/Ohio-State/Football/2015/News/For-Ohio-State-Nine-Units-Strong-is-the-Goal-Everything-Else-is-Inertia

Harris, G. (n.d.). *What is the DISC Model?* Retrieved from DISC Personality Testing: https://discpersonalitytesting.com/blog/what-is-the-disc-model/

Hartman, J. (2014, May 22). *The Steelers draft process is all about the 'vision'.* Retrieved from Behind the Steel Curtain: http://www.behindthesteelcurtain.com/2014-nfl-draft/2014/5/22/5741120/steelers-draft-review-video-espn-2014

Heinz, W. (Director). (1967). *The Science and Art of Football* [Motion Picture].

Heinz, W. (Director). (1967). *The Science and Art of Football* [Motion Picture].

Heisler, Y. (2014, May 20). *What ever became of Microsoft's $150 million investment in Apple?* Retrieved from Engadget.com: https://www.engadget.com/2014/05/20/what-ever-became-of-microsofts-150-million-investment-in-apple/

Heskett, J., Sasser, W., & Schlesinger, L. (1997). *The Service Profit Chain.* Free Press.

Heskett, J., Schlesinger, L., Sasser, W., Jones, T., & Loveman, G. (2008, July). Putting the Service Profit Chain to Work. *Harvard Business Review.*

Hoffman, B. (2012, March 12). Saving an Iconic Brand: Five Ways Alan Mulally Changed Ford's Culture. *Fast Company.*

Holtz, L., & McCormick, B. (2007, May). *Lou Holtz, National Leader of the Month, May 2007.* Retrieved from Leader Network: http://www.leadernetwork.org/lou_holtz_may_07.htm

Hull, P. (2012, December 19). *Be Visionary. Think Big.* Retrieved from Forbes: https://www.forbes.com/sites/patrickhull/2012/12/19/be-visionary-think-big/#1efe33283c17

Ilkin, T., & Williams, D. (2014). *Forged in Steel.* Beaver, Pennsylvania: Minerd Publishing.

Investopedia. (2015, June 10). *How Is Southwest Different From Other Airlines?* Retrieved from Investopedia: http://www.investopedia.com/articles/investing/061015/how-southwest-different-other-airlines.asp

Isaac, M. (2017, June 13). Uber Embraces Major Reforms as Travis Kalanick, the C.E.O., Steps Away. *New York Times.*

Jackson, Z. (2016, January 10). *Steelers saved by Bengals' penalties, Boswell field goal.* Retrieved from Pro Football Talk: http://profootballtalk.nbcsports.com/2016/01/10/steelers-saved-by-bengals-penalties-boswell-field-goal/

Jhonsa, E. (2017, April 26). *Here's How T-Mobile Is Winning Subscribers Away From Verizon and AT&T.* Retrieved from The Street: https://www.thestreet.com/story/14103441/1/here-s-how-t-mobile-is-winning-market-share-from-verizon-at-amp-t.html

Jones, G., & Schneider, W. J. (2006). *IQ in the Production Function: Evidence from Immigrant Earnings.* Edwardsville: Southern Illinois University.

Kaplan, R. S. (2005). Creating the Office of Strategy Management. 1.

Karp, H. (2009, December 17). Texas Football Boosters Think Big. *Wall Street Journal.*

Kerr, J. (2015, January 26). How Bill Belichick's 'Do Your Job' Mantra Applies to Leadership. *Inc.*

Kotter, J., & Heskett, J. (1992). *Corporate Culture and Performance.* Free Press.

Kraemer, H. (2015, June 18). *How Ford CEO Alan Mullaly turned a broken company into the industry's comeback kid.* Retrieved from Quartz: https://qz.com/431078/how-ford-ceo-alan-mullaly-turned-a-broken-company-into-the-industrys-comeback-kid/

Layden, T. (2010). *Blood, Sweat and Chalk.* Simmsbury, CT: Sports Illustrated Books.

Learned, E. P. (1969). *Business Policy: Text & Cases.* R.D. Irwin.

Mankins, M. (2013). The Defining Elements of a Winning Culture. *Harvard Business Review.*

Mccord, P. (2014). How Netflix Reinvented HR. *Harvard Business Review.*

Meyer, D. (1952). *Spread Formation Football.* Prentice Hall.

Meyer, U. (2015). *Above the Line: Lesson in Leadership and Life from a Championship Season.* Penguin.

News, A. R. (2015). *Market Data - US Rental Car Market.*

NFL, F. (1982, January 10). *The Catch.* Retrieved from nfl.com: http://www.nfl.com/videos/san-francisco-49ers/0ap3000000674219/Top-50-Fantasy-Show-32-Carlos-Hyde

O'Keefe, B. (2012, September 7). *Leadership Lessons from Alabama football coach Nick Saban.* Retrieved from Fortune: http://fortune.com/2012/09/07/leadership-lessons-from-alabama-football-coach-nick-saban/

Olson, M. (2013, December 7). *Brown was a recruiting game-changer.* Retrieved from ESPN: http://espn.go.com/college-sports/recruiting/football/story/_/id/10152888/texas-longhorns-coach-mack-brown-changed-game-recruiting

Onetto, M. (2009, October 20). *Mark A. Onetto, Senior Vice President of Worldwide Operations and Customer Service, Amazon.com, Inc.* Retrieved from YouTube: https://www.youtube.com/watch?v=Foy1FTBjHK4

Pace, J. (n.d.). *How to Prepare for a Job Interview or Big Meeting.* Retrieved from The Pacific Institute: http://thepacificinstitute.com/blog/2014/01/13/how-to-prepare-for-a-job-interview-or-big-meeting/

Packard, D. (2006). *The HP Way: How Bill Hewlett and I Built Our Company (reprint).* HarperBusiness.

Press, A. (1993, October 19). *Cutting-Room Floor : Roper Released After Snoozing During Film.* Retrieved from Los Angeles Times: http://articles.latimes.com/1993-10-19/sports/sp-47408_1_vinson-smith

Pro Football Reference. (1982, January 10). *Dallas Cowboys at San Francisco 49ers - January 10th, 1982.* Retrieved from Pro-Football-Reference.com: http://www.pro-football-reference.com/boxscores/198201100sfo.htm#all_team_stats

Quinn, R., & Cameron, K. (2006). *Diagnosing and Changing Organizational Culture.* San Francisco: Jossey-Bass.

Reference, P. F. (n.d.). *Jonas Gray.* Retrieved from Pro Football Reference.com: https://www.pro-football-reference.com/players/G/GrayJo00/gamelog/2014/

Reiss, M. (2014, December 18). *What makes the Pats offense unique?* Retrieved from Espn.com: http://www.espn.com/nfl/story/_/id/12039309/experts-makes-new-engalnd-patriots-offense-unique

Rishe, P. (2013, December 15). The Finances of Mack Brown's Impact. *Forbes.*

Schefter, A., & Shanahan, M. (1999). *Think Like a Champion: Building Success One Victory at a Time.* HarperBusiness.

Schlappig, B. (2016, June 15). *My Experience Switching from AT&T to T-Mobile.* Retrieved from One Mile at a Time: http://onemileatatime.boardingarea.com/2016/06/15/switching-att-tmobile/

Spence, R., & Rushing, H. (n.d.). *It's Not What You Sell, It's What You Stand For.* Austin.

Staff, N. Y. (2011, January 31). The "Steeler Way" works. *New York Post.*

Steelers, P. (Perpetual). *Pittsburgh Steelers Mission Statement.* Retrieved from PittsburghSteelers.com: http://www.steelers.com/community/mission-statement.html

Tully , S. (2015, September 23). *Southwest bets big on business travelers.* Retrieved from Fortune.com: http://fortune.com/2015/09/23/southwest-airlines-business-travel/

Various. (2015, September 29). *The Catch (American Football).* Retrieved from Wikipedia: https://en.wikipedia.org/w/index.php?title=The_Catch_(American_football)&action=history

Various. (2017). *VMware.* Retrieved from Wikipedia: https://en.wikipedia.org/wiki/VMware

Various. (n.d.). *Bill Parcells.* Retrieved from Wikipedia.org: https://en.wikipedia.org/wiki/Bill_Parcells

Various. (n.d.). *Cleveland Browns relocation controversy.* Retrieved from Wikipedia.org: https://en.wikipedia.org/wiki/Cleveland_Browns_relocation_controversy

Various. (n.d.). *Cognition.* Retrieved from Wikipedia: https://en.wikipedia.org/wiki/Cognition

Various. (n.d.). *Composite NFL records since the AFL merged into the NFL in 1970.* Retrieved from JPS.net: http://home.jps.net/~fos/nfl/post1969nfl.html

Various. (n.d.). *History of Southwest Airlines.* Retrieved from Wikipedia.org: https://en.wikipedia.org/wiki/History_of_Southwest_Airlines

Various. (n.d.). *Lake Travis High School Football.* Retrieved from Wikipedia: https://en.wikipedia.org/wiki/Lake_Travis_High_School#Football

Various. (n.d.). *Michael Dell.* Retrieved from Wikipedia: https://en.wikipedia.org/wiki/Michael_Dell

Various. (n.d.). *Moore's Law.* Retrieved from Wikipedia: https://en.wikipedia.org/wiki/Moore%27s_law

Various. (Perpetual). *Salary Cap: National Football League.* Retrieved from Wikipedia: https://en.wikipedia.org/wiki/Salary_cap#National_Football_League

Various. (n.d.). *Syracuse Orange Football.* Retrieved from Wikipedia: https://en.wikipedia.org/wiki/Syracuse_Orange_football

Various. (n.d.). *T Mobile US.* Retrieved from Wikipedia.org: https://en.wikipedia.org/wiki/T-Mobile_US#The_.22Un-carrier.22.2C_additional_wireless_spectrum_acquisition

Various. (n.d.). *Texas Longhorns Football Under Mack Brown.* Retrieved from Wikipedia: https://en.wikipedia.org/wiki/Texas_Longhorns_football_under_Mack_Brown

Various. (n.d.). *The Catch (American Football).* Retrieved from Wikipedia: https://en.wikipedia.org/wiki/The_Catch_(American_football)

Various. (n.d.). *Urban Meyer.* Retrieved from Wikipedia: https://en.wikipedia.org/wiki/Urban_Meyer#Bowling_Green

Various. (n.d.). *Vitality Curve.* Retrieved from Wikipedia: https://en.wikipedia.org/wiki/Vitality_curve

Walker, J. (2011, May 10). *Rooney family, Steelers have special culture.* Retrieved from ESPN.com: http://espn.go.com/blog/afcnorth/post/_/id/27448/rooney-family-steelers-have-special-culture

Walsh, B. (2009). *The Score Takes Care of Itself: My Philosophy of Leadership.* New York, NY: Penguin.

Walsh, B., & Billick, B. (1997). *Finding the Winning Edge.* Sports Publishing.

Walsh, C. (2017, April 21). *Nick Saban explains his frustration with proposed rule banning high school coaches from camps.* Retrieved from SEC Country: https://www.seccountry.com/alabama/nick-saban-explains-frustration-new-rule-banning-high-school-coaches-camps

Watkins, M. (2003). *The First 90 Days.* Boston: Harvard Business School Publishing.

Weihrich, H. (1982). *The TOWS Matrix - A Tool for Situational Analysis.* Retrieved from The University of San Francisco: http://www.rillo.ee/docs/2008/Weichrich_LRP_1982.pdf

Welch, J. (2003). *Straight from the Gut.* Grand Central.

Whitaker, T., & Gruenert, S. (2015). *School Culture Rewired: How to Define, Assess, and Transform It.* ASCD.

Wikipedia, V. (n.d.). *Wikipedia - Joe Jamail*. Retrieved November 2, 2013, from Wikipedia.org: http://en.wikipedia.org/wiki/Joe_Jamail

Wojciechowsk, G. (2012, December 12). *Top 10 coaching jobs in college football*. Retrieved November 2, 2013, from ESPN.com: http://espn. go.com/college-football/story/_/id/8733842/from-nfl-college-ranking-10-best-head-coaching-jobs-football-college-football

CPSIA information can be obtained
at www.ICGtesting.com
Printed in the USA
BVOW06*1624191217
503082BV00003B/8/P

9 780999 644126